DISCARD

HELP

FOR THE

HURTING HEART

A CHRISTIAN PERSPECTIVE FOR
THOSE WHO HAVE LEARNED
THAT FORGIVING AND FORGETTING
DOESN'T WORK

JUL -- 2014

DISCARD

HELP

FOR THE

HURTING
HEART

A CHRISTIAN PERSPECTIVE FOR
THOSE WHO HAVE LEARNED
THAT FORGIVING AND FORGETTING
DOESN'T WORK

Dr. Steven R. Silverstein

TATE PUBLISHING
AND ENTERPRISES, LLC

Help for the Hurting Heart
Copyright © 2012 by Dr. Steven R. Silverstein. All rights reserved.

No part of this publication may be reproduced, stored in a retrieval system or transmitted in any way by any means, electronic, mechanical, photocopy, recording or otherwise without the prior permission of the author except as provided by USA copyright law.

Scriptures taken from the Holy Bible, New International Version®, niv®. Copyright © 1973, 1978, 1984 by Biblica, Inc.™ Used by permission of Zondervan. All rights reserved worldwide. www.zondervan.com

The opinions expressed by the author are not necessarily those of Tate Publishing, LLC.

This book is designed to provide accurate and authoritative information with regard to the subject matter covered. This information is given with the understanding that neither the author nor Tate Publishing, LLC is engaged in rendering legal, professional advice. Since the details of your situation are fact dependent, you should additionally seek the services of a competent professional. The opinions expressed by the author are not necessarily those of Tate Publishing, LLC.

Published by Tate Publishing & Enterprises, LLC

127 E. Trade Center Terrace | Mustang, Oklahoma 73064 USA
1.888.361.9473 | www.tatepublishing.com

Tate Publishing is committed to excellence in the publishing industry. The company reflects the philosophy established by the founders, based on Psalm 68:11,

"The Lord gave the word and great was the company of those who published it."

Book design copyright © 2012 by Tate Publishing, LLC. All rights reserved.
Cover design by Nathan Harmony
Interior design by Glenn Rico Orat
Published in the United States of America

ISBN: 978-1-62024-670-2
Self-Help / Spiritual
Religion / Christian Life / Social Issues
12.10.03

"I love this book because its words are so caring and understanding. As I read, I felt safe and comforted so that it was much easier to deal with my feelings. The only thing more comforting to me through the years has been the Psalms."

Kari Ann Kinkey
DeFuniak Springs, Florida

"I was talking to my sister who has ruined her life a few times. She has struggled with a girl at work, and the whole situation has made her extremely bitter. She called me (the baby of the family) for advice. I told her after quite a bit of listening, that she hadn't really forgiven the girl. It was quite obvious to me. Before I knew it, I was reciting the Internal Evidences of Healing. I told her I had a book for her to read. She didn't sound totally convinced, but I took it to her anyway. She called me back the other day. She is almost done with Help For The Hurting Heart. She loves it and is using the worksheets. She has learned a great deal. Her life has taken a 180-degree turn – now if it will just stay that way. I just thought that I would share the impact this book has had in one life. And seeing the change that I have been praying for, for eight years, has changed my life. Thanks!"

Elizabeth Buckwalter
Scranton, Pennsylvania

The Hurting Heart Checklist

Who needs this book? How can someone tell? Consider the following.

____True ____False   I am told I am too sensitive.

____True ____False   I feel anxious and worried.

____True ____False   I feel sad and depressed.

____True ____False   I feel unimportant.

____True ____False   I feel inadequate and guilty.

____True ____False   I feel unloved.

____True ____False   I am told I overreact.

____True ____False   I am told I am controlling.

____True ____False   I become angry quickly and severely.

____True ____False   I feel empty inside.

____True ____False   I find it difficult to trust people.

____True ____False   I tend to hold grudges.

____True ____False   I try to live up to certain expectations.

____True ____False   I look for approval from people.

____True ____False   I struggle with being open and honest about personal things.

____True ____False   I struggle with knowing and maintaining healthy boundaries.

____True ____False   I avoid certain people because of past incidents.

How many of these statements are true of you? Better yet, how many of these statements do you want to be true of you? Some say these statements are too general. Others say everyone feels like this at times. Not true. Are these characteristics normal? No, but they might be surprisingly common. If they are typical for you, it is not a healthy norm.

This is a journey of personal growth. The journey of Help for the Hurting Heart will help you progress from where you are now to find a healthy norm where these statements can become false.

Statement of Confidentiality

It is essential in the field of counseling to protect confidentiality. The names and particular details of certain stories within this book have been altered. This protects those who were willing to share their experience as well as those who were formerly indebted to them.

For additional information about Dr. Steven R. Silverstein and his speaking schedule, lecture series, and biblical counseling ministry with Alternatives in Counseling, Inc. or additional copies of this book, you may use the web at AlternativesInCounseling.webs.com, write, or call:

Dr. Steven R. Silverstein, ACS, LPC, LCADC
c/o Alternatives in Counseling, Inc.
212 Barclay Pavilion East
Cherry Hill, NJ 08034
570-905-4290

Dedication

To those who are hurting deeply but have not yet started on the healing journey of forgiveness, may God's strength and courage become your own so you may take those crucial first steps. To those who have just recently taken your first steps, may God's comforting love begin to soothe your pain and heal your hurting heart.

To all who are somewhere farther along on the journey, may we continue together.

To those who pioneered the journey of forgiveness so we can stand on your shoulders and see farther ahead on our own journey, we find you faithful and we are grateful.

Acknowledgments

To my dear Lord. I want to express my gratitude for your abundant grace and mercy upon my life. It is with greatest thanks and appreciation that I acknowledge what You have done and what You are doing in my life. Truly, I am humbled and privileged to participate in Your glorious work of healing the hurting heart and reconciling and restoring relationships.

To my wife and sweetheart, Kathy, and to our children: Jason, Annette, Emily, and Evelyn. You have taught me much and helped me enormously on this journey. Without your sacrifice and encouragement, this book would not be possible.

To Debbie Yurevich, thank you for your unique and wonderful giftedness and partnership in this work. Your discernment, expertise, and countless hours of dedication have been vital.

To Kari Ann Kinkey, Carol King, Debbie Nichols, Barry and Sarah Phillips, and Diana Sollars. Your contributions made this book clearer, more concise, and complete. You have my warmest thanks.

TABLE OF CONTENTS

PART ONE: KNOWLEDGE

PART TWO: UNDERSTANDING

PART THREE: WISDOM

APPENDICES

Preface

Please take a moment to let me share with you my intent and purpose for writing this book. I believe understanding my heart up front will greatly influence the way you read and benefit from this work about forgiveness.

The purpose of *Help for the Hurting Heart* is to motivate and guide you to understand and overcome the negative effects of hurtful relationships. I have worked to be simple and maintain biblical accuracy while removing the mask of religion.

The content of these pages is primarily a practical work. This book has been modified in other forms for use in small groups and as lectures for larger group presentations.

The first motive is to help that person who is holding onto resentments and is currently unable to enjoy the benefits of forgiveness because he or she doesn't understand the meaning of forgiveness. It is my prayer that this work be clear and practical for any hurting person to fully understand the journey of forgiveness.

It is critical to know whether or not you have received God's forgiveness for your own sinfulness. Although this is not a book focused on salvation, unless you have experienced God's forgiveness through the Messiah, Jesus Christ, you will not be able to truly forgive others.

The aim of this book is that of resolving and healing personal relationship issues. *Help for the Hurting Heart* will take you to the place of learning to recognize, repair, and rebuild personal relationships that have been damaged throughout your lifetime. Learning how to express forgiveness to others is essential for the sake of your relationship with Jesus Christ, for your spiritual and emotional well-being, and for the enjoyment of your relationships with other people.

This book is intended to provide a clear definition of biblical forgiveness. Forgiveness is commonly discussed as though everyone already knows what it means and as if the reader is unwilling to forgive. People do experience a natural resistance to offering and receiving forgiveness. I attempt to give you practical understanding and principles to help you overcome resistance and choose to forgive by faith even when you don't feel like forgiving. My intention is to clearly present forgiveness side by side with all of the issues that are usually confused with true forgiveness. Some of these issues include forgetting, reconciling, restitution, and restoration of a relationship.

You might choose to read this book one chapter at a time, taking patient and persistent action as you go. You might decide to read through the book completely first and then prayerfully follow God's prompting to act on its principles. I do not encourage skipping around. The journey is built on a progressive foundation. Missing critical elements in the foundation can lead to serious difficulties that hinder and complicate the easiest route of this journey, causing additional misery. You may benefit by reading it a second time. Work through the exercises, journal your thoughts and feelings, and write down the statements that pop off the page and speak to you personally. There is no rush, but there is a sense of urgency because your well-being is important. Choose whatever method works for you. Move at God's pace for your life.

Finally, this book is presented in a format meant to guide and support you as you grow throughout the experience of forgiveness. The signs of progress are clearly identifiable along the journey. You will read about the experiences of others, and I hope these experiences will help you in many ways along your own journey.

Just as your progress will be easy to see, I hope it will also be easy to see if you are living a life full of unforgiveness. I will give you clear indicators for determining if the spirit of unforgiveness is a reality in your life. I will also give you insight on how to know if your life displays evidence of the abundant life that Christ's death and forgiveness provide for you.

I express my sincerest appreciation to you for taking time to read *Help for the Hurting Heart*. I trust that God will richly bless this book so that it is a genuine help and enduring blessing to you.

Gratefully,
Steve Silverstein

> "And be ye kind one to another, tenderhearted, forgiving one another, even as God for Christ's sake hath forgiven you" (Ephesians 4:32).

PART ONE: KNOWLEDGE

"The fear of the Lord is the beginning of knowledge: but fools despise wisdom and instruction" (Proverbs 1:7).

My prayer is that your sadness, depression, anxiety, pain, or confusion leads you to the knowledge of truth. May you bring your broken spirit and wounded soul to our loving God for His gracious healing. I pray that you will worship and glorify Him. May His truth heal your broken spirit and restore your wounded soul.

WE'RE GOING ON A JOURNEY

Christine's mom screamed at her and pushed her across the kitchen to her dad. He got up from the table and shoved Christine back to her mom, all the while screaming in her face. Trapped between them, she flew back and forth. The yelling continued, each parent reinforcing the other's brutal remarks to Christine. Dad pushed her violently, and she fell onto the stone hearth. Back up again, Christine was hit on her legs and back as she flinched back around, trying to avoid the physical punishment. Her mom caught her by her hair, yanked her backward, and jerked her around. She was pushed. She was thrown. She desperately tried to back away to escape to her bedroom but couldn't. Instead she was knocked onto the coffee table. They pulled her up and continued to shove her. This time, she hit the lamp. The lamp hit the floor. *Surely now this will stop,* she thought. Finally, she found herself lying on the floor, helpless, crying. It was over.

On the floor, along with her stunned thirteen-year-old mind, battered body, and shattered emotions, was the teacher's letter. It stated that Christine disrespected her teacher, who called her a little witch. The note required that she write a paragraph vowing never to be disrespectful again. Somehow, she managed to bring herself back to reality as she heard her parents tell her to get up and go to her room. Stunned and hurting, Christine picked up herself and the paper from the kitchen floor. She walked cautiously to her room only to hear her parents tell her she "better never pull something like this again."

Christine was hurting. She still loved her parents. She wanted them to love her. She wanted to feel loved. She wanted to feel loveable. Christine was Daddy's girl. She wondered for days whether or not her daddy was still mad at her for what she did. She felt afraid that he didn't love her anymore. The physical beating was over, but she couldn't forget the yelling and screaming. She walked on eggshells. Now she longed for her parents to forgive her. She desperately longed for things to get back to normal at her house. Things didn't return to normal. They grew worse.

A few years later, she wanted to forgive her parents. It was the right thing to do. But what is forgiveness?

How would you respond if you were in Christine's shoes? The treatment might have been less devastating than some other abuse, yet the heart wounds penetrated and are as deep as anyone could experience.

"I'll never forgive him."

"I'm not ready yet."

"I think I did already."

Anger and pain are often present with the familiar statements. They can be said with a feeling of inferiority or an air of superiority. Regardless, these words and feelings reveal the struggle you face when you consider forgiving those who brutally injured, carelessly neglected, or totally misunderstood you.

"I'm supposed to forgive."

"I want to forgive."

"I don't know how to forgive!"

Comments like these might reflect the confusion you feel. They might be the reason you lack closeness in the most personal and sensitive area of your life: your relationships. All of us sincerely want love, warmth, and intimacy in our relationships, but many cannot give or receive it.

This Journey Might Not Be For You

There are some people who do not appear to struggle with healing from injuries in life. Corrie Ten Boom was such a person. The author of *The Hiding Place*, Corrie was a survivor of the Nazi concentration camps. During her years in captivity, she endured horrible atrocities. Many view her as an amazing woman. Many underestimate how terrible it really was because she healed so well. It seems as though she healed easier than others, but this was not the case.

The survivors of the concentration camps were permanently scarred by the experience. Some were physically maimed. Emotional wounds had an enormous impact on the rest of their lives. Numerous survivors were so traumatized they were never capable of fully functioning again. Corrie told her story. But many could not discuss the horror of their memories.

All people are unique and thus respond uniquely to life's sufferings. Ten million people suffered torture and murder in concentration camps. Some of the survivors, who witnessed the horror, never healed from the trauma. They still struggle with healing and forgiveness. Others healed without much lasting impact on their lives as a whole. People might have very similar injuries and experiences yet respond in different ways.

If you recover easily from traumatic events, you might be the kind of person who does not experience a struggle with forgiveness. This journey might be easier for you. You might not even understand, appreciate, or feel compassion for those who do not recover so easily and experience a greater struggle with forgiveness.

The following comparison might help those who struggle to understand. Some people have allergies, and others do not. Those who do not have allergies cannot fully appreciate the suffering of those who have them. Emotional sensitivity is not a disease, but the lack of understanding is a real issue. Many of God's children are deeply sensitive and have genuine struggles with healing and forgiveness. The ability to forgive seems more like a fairy tale or myth rather than the truth of God. The journey of forgiveness described in this book is for those who need and want help. This journey will be a life-transforming reality for those who receive help from the biblical principles presented in these pages.

Where Is God in All of This?

Where is God? Is there a God? If so, then why did He let this happen to Christine? Does He even care about her, or you?

Many people struggle to have a relationship with God. They might find similar difficulty in their close relationships with people. Until you have truly experienced God's love in personal and practical ways, you will not be able to truly love Him and others. Therefore, you might not be able to make any sense out of life's problems. You might even hold resentments against God. This is because God set up relationships that we must first know His forgiveness and love Him, and then we will be able to forgive and love others.

"Love the Lord your God with all your heart and with all your soul and with all your strength" (Deuteronomy 6:5).

"Jesus replied: 'Love the Lord your God with all your heart and with all your soul and with all your mind.' This is the first and greatest commandment. And the second is like it: 'Love your neighbor as yourself. All the Law and the Prophets hang on these two commandments'" (Matthew 22:37-40).

God has provided forgiveness so that we can enjoy a relationship with Him. His forgiveness also provides an example to follow. Our ability to reach a deeper level of intimacy in relationships with others is directly impacted by our willingness to offer, express, and accept forgiveness. In relationships, love, joy, peace, and intimacy are the result of genuine forgiveness extended between two people.

"Forgive us our debts, as we also have forgiven our debtors" (Matthew 6:12).

I frequently hear people mention and discuss forgiveness in their conversations. I am convinced that partial or inaccurate explanations and concepts lacking the full truth have led many astray into deeper confusion, frustration, and pain. There appears to be little accurate thought, knowledge, and understanding about the meaning of forgiveness and its role in developing intimate relationships.

Forgiveness is not a complicated process. This is not to say it is easy, but it is not complicated. We hinder the effect of biblical forgiveness by believing that it must be complicated in order to be effective. I often use an illustration from building our swimming pool; a generous family gave our younger family a large above-ground pool because their children had grown. The catch was that I would have to prepare the ground. Unfortunately, I had to excavate the sloping backyard by hand and then shovel and wheelbarrow the truckload of sand from the driveway. This was not complicated, but it was very hard to do during the summer heat wave. And in the same way, forgiveness can be very challenging.

We must be careful not to confuse or add to what God has established, provided, and commanded in His Word. Our human nature goes against forgiveness; that is what makes it so challenging. Nevertheless, what is difficult and impossible with us is possible with God. By faith, we can choose to apply what Jesus teaches in the Scripture about forgiveness. Faith choices will call us to a higher place of trust in Christ. We can cancel the debt.

Children are a wonderful example of how simple it really is to forgive. You might ask, "Do children truly forgive?" Let us look at the following situation to demonstrate an accurate understanding of forgiveness.

Susie and Jenny were playing with their dolls when Susie decided she wanted to be mommy to the doll in the pink blanket. This would not be a problem except that Jenny already chose this doll as her own baby. She was not willing to give her baby doll up for adoption so easily. Before long, the babysitter heard the commotion in the playroom and came to rescue the doll in the pink blanket from having its plastic head and stubby feet pulled off in the tug-of-war. The wise babysitter listened carefully to each girl tell her side of the story and express her hurt feelings. She then helped each one see her responsibility in the conflict. In this moment, Susie and Jenny wiped the tears away. Each little girl, of her own free will, demonstrated genuine sorrow and a willingness to change. They began to play in peace and harmony together again. This is biblical forgiveness at its best.

This situation would have ended differently if they were instructed to apologize and hug each other without addressing the hurt that was involved. The well-meaning sitter would have given them, even in this most elementary illustration, an inaccurate picture of the truth about forgiveness. They likely would have taken this "hug and make up" view of forgiveness with them throughout their life and replayed it over and over again in their relationships with others. This misunderstanding would have placed them in an emotional and spiritual prison, which would hold them captive. When hurts are not addressed, they can be stored within the person. Unresolved pain can become resentment and eventually bitterness. Forgiveness is an issue of the heart. Determining responsibility and allowing release makes it possible to avoid resentment and bitterness.

Many sincere, well-meaning people present an incomplete explanation of forgiveness because they do not fully understand true forgiveness. Lack of understanding, even with pure motives, leads to more agony and a sense of hopelessness.

It is my hope to present a clear, complete, and biblically accurate picture of the journey toward genuine forgiveness in relationships. We will focus on practical ways to apply and experience the forgiveness we receive from God, through the cross of Jesus Christ, in our relationships with others. Only then can we begin to experience the intimacy we desire in all of our relationships.

"For if you forgive men when they sin against you, your heavenly Father will also forgive you. But if you do not forgive men their sins, your Father will not forgive your sins" (Matthew 6:14-15).

Well-Meaning Misconceptions

Let's identify some of the most common misconceptions to help focus on the true meaning of forgiveness.

Well-meaning people frequently advise others to "forgive and forget." This advice cannot soothe your pain. Some have suggested that time heals all wounds, but this is absolutely not true. The intensity of the immediate pain might subside, but genuine healing requires cleansing of the wound, setting the broken bone straight, along with therapy. Infection, more serious injury, and pain can occur if proper treatment does not happen. Trying to forget adds frustration to your already-aching heart because no matter how hard you try, you cannot forget. This idea has been compared to forgetting that you were in an accident where you lost an arm or leg. You just cannot forget something like this. God never intended for you to forget. The Scriptures often encourage us to remember. The advice to forgive and forget creates a major problem because you can't put the disturbing thoughts and feelings about the incident out of your mind. Some suggest that since you can't forget, then you didn't really forgive.

Common Misunderstandings

If I can't forget, I didn't forgive.

If I forgive, I can't acknowledge the offense to anyone.

If it doesn't feel comfortable, I must not be doing the right thing.

If things look hopeless, they must be.

Forgiveness is not forgetting, although you might wish you could erase the tragedy, horror, and pain from your mind. Forgiveness does not minimize or dismiss the event or its consequences. In fact, acknowledging the offense and its results is part of the journey of true forgiveness.

Resisting the Journey of Forgiveness

The arguments to resist the journey of forgiveness can explode within your mind and leave you paralyzed. Take a look at the following list to determine the arguments you may be using to avoid forgiving someone.

Common Arguments

I just can't!

I'm terrified when I think about her.

But she would only hurt me again.

But she is old, and it was a long time ago.

This is just high school stuff.

I don't get it. What's the point?

There is no hope. It doesn't matter anymore.

My answer to these arguments is: you can forgive. It's okay to feel scared when you think about her. Yes, she might hurt you again, but that doesn't negate your need to forgive. It does not matter that he is old or that this hurtful event happened a long time ago. It is not just high school stuff; this has bothered you for years. There is a point to it all. There is hope, and it does matter. When you replace faulty thinking with a clear, biblical understanding of forgiveness, you begin to experience forgiveness and benefit from its healing. There is hope in Christ.

The Biblical Definition of Forgiveness

Matthew 18 contains clear teaching on forgiveness. Sinful actions affect people, their relationships, and create a spiritual debt.[1] God longs for the restoring of relationships.[2] The closing parable illustrates the forgiving of a debt that cannot be repaid.[3] Forgiveness is a financial term that simply means "to cancel the debt." Biblical forgiveness conveys to the offender that there has been a debt, and, "Since I have forgiven you, you no longer owe a debt to me; the debt has been cancelled."

Another aspect of forgiveness recognizes that God is just. We acknowledge His justice and come to the place where we trust Him to remedy the situation and resolve the debt. We do not need to understand how or when God will do this. We learn that God is faithful, sovereign, and worthy to be trusted. Genuine and simple faith is essential on our part.

The Value of a Debt

An offense creates a debt within the heart of the offended person. Every debt has a specific value. The offended party must recognize the value of the debt in order to do the work of the debt through the act of forgiveness. The Messiah, Jesus Christ, paid the great debt of sin, which we all owe and cannot pay ourselves. The gift of salvation gives us an opportunity to experience the forgiveness of our sin debt. This gives spiritual freedom in order to have a relationship with God and others.

As you become ready to begin this journey, keep the biblical view of forgiveness in mind. Realize that even though it might seem impossible to forgive, the alternative is much worse. Unforgiveness leads to bitterness, more brokenness, and a life of regret.

A Time for Reflection

1. How would you explain what it means to forgive?

2. Express how you have personally experienced God's forgiveness.

3. Describe a time when you realized you needed to forgive someone, but you struggled to do so.

Why You Must (and Why You Might Not) Take the Journey

Why consider this difficult journey of forgiveness? We all need relief from pain and suffering caused in relationships. Critics have said, "Relationships are not worth the trouble," "They drag me down," "They require more effort than they are worth." It seems impossible to imagine a safe relationship. Enriching relationships seem beyond comprehension for some. Yet, there is a longing to love and be loved, but relationships can be so hurtful.

Why is there so much hurt in relationships? Is the world filled with malicious people? Are people just stupid? What is it? Children are naturally self-centered. As they grow, conflicts are inevitable. During the maturing process, they should begin to understand and develop social skills. When selfishness persists, the results become obvious. Awareness and acceptance of others prevent damaging arguments. The lack of understanding causes much damage.

It is embarrassing to admit my own insensitivity and ignorance toward my wife and family. The all-too-common scenario of getting to church on time is a very real and painful memory. My priority was getting to church early enough to greet, chit chat, find the right pew, be settled, and meditate before the first hymn. This seemed very reasonable and the righteous thing to do.

"I hate being late. You need to get up earlier. If you do not get up the first time I call you, I will get the water. Why can't you have the children ready on time? I am so embarrassed when we walk in after church has started. I will leave without you!"

As fate (and God) would have it, my wife had a very different perspective. "You know if you would just help, instead of complaining. They are just children. Things happen. I can only do so much. Please, just leave."

Degrading comments, criticism, frustration, and tears filled many car rides to church before I would greet visitors with smiling love and grace. Eventually, God ripped away my stubborn pride and arrogance and convinced me of my hypocritical self-righteousness. My behavior needed to change, and my wife needed understanding, support, and freedom to express her frustration and disappointment. I needed forgiveness and mercy from God and my family.

Understanding

In order to grow towards proper understanding of people, it would help to avoid these damaging conflicts. This requires a change of thinking from self-absorption to that of love and other centered selflessness. Not easy! It requires intentional effort and lots of practice. This is change, growth, maturity.

Each person is unique with his or her own set of qualities, characteristics, and priorities. These personal attributes are distinct and not in conflict with God's moral law. God determines moral values and timeless truths for all. Breaking God's laws causes conflict. Selfishness and the lack of understanding of personal differences is a source of relational conflict. These misunderstandings are not moral issues but that of diversity. Consideration and respect for personal differences would eliminate these clashes.

Understanding diversity means that some prefer the security of routine while others become bored and enjoy the pleasures of adventure. Some are effective managers while others are pioneers and visionaries. There are those who have learned to save for the rainy day and contrast with those who believe it is important to live life today. Understanding and balance is essential for harmony.

The pain feels different for each of us. It is personal, stressful, and sometimes overwhelming. Your damaged relationship can bring out emotions such as anger and bitterness. These undesirable feelings are usually considered *bad*. You might try to avoid *bad* feelings at all costs. Yet, pain can be beneficial *if* it motivates you to do the right things. When you realize that your distress indicates the presence of a wound, I hope you will want to find relief and healing.

Feelings

Feelings are peculiar things. Understanding and managing them can be very challenging. Sometimes, they manage us. Some people are emotionally numb. They know they are feeling something but cannot identify it. There are those who cannot sense their own pain. Often, people need help to express their pain. At first, it might seem irrelevant, foolish, or dangerous to try to express your emotions. Feelings need to be expressed, acknowledged, understood, and accepted for a mutual healthy relationship. Many have been wrongly taught that their feelings are bad, mistaken, and untrustworthy. This is never true. Feelings are what they are, just feelings.

There are many emotions, and certain ones are very undesirable, but they are not necessarily bad nor good.

They are given birth out of our thoughts, behaviors, and circumstances. For example, no one longs to be sad, but sometimes sad is very appropriate. This is true when a favorite pet passes away. Expressing sadness is very important and helpful in grieving.

There is always a time when you will need to feel, label, and express your emotions. Families commonly teach us to shut down our emotions. They accuse us of being over-sensitive. We develop coping behaviors to protect ourselves. Therefore, we learn to be counterfeit rather than authentic. Changing this pattern takes time and is very difficult. Often people need help to become genuine. If you need assistance with labeling your feelings, reviewing the "Glossary of Feelings" included at the end of this book will help you identify where you are on the journey.

Coping Behaviors

In the following pages, we will explore several unhealthy coping behaviors and attitudes that are used to manage the emotional and spiritual ache that follows an injury. These reactions are used to avoid pain when (and after) we experience an offense. Families adopt behavior patterns in order to cope. They respond to situations in predictable patterns. It can be easy to notice the coping behaviors of others. One parent might act like a maniac while the other plays the victim. Recognizing these traits in ourselves might be much more challenging. Coping behaviors can be described as the martyr, the maniac, and the mean person.

Coping Behaviors

The Martyr: depression, "poor me," whining, complaining, manipulation.

The Maniac: rage, compulsion, obsessions, indulgence.

The Mean Person: intolerant, sarcastic, belittling, blame shifting.

These behaviors, though common, never bring healing and freedom. They cause more distress. These behavioral patterns only serve to bring a self-defeating and dysfunctional family and lifestyle. Jesus came to provide an abundant life far different from this.

Rationalizations

Avoiding pain and resolving conflict can seem impossible. Many assume this sort of life as normal for all and unconsciously rationalize acceptance in order to survive. These are considered normal responses to life's experiences. Ways to rationalize past history includes:

Rationalizations

Self-deception: "It never happened."

Self-denial: "There is no pain."

Self-destruction: "I can pretend the pain was never there."

Self-delusion: "The hurt is not that bad."

Self-degradation: "I am not worthy to feel my true feelings.

Self-deception: "It never happened."

Self-deception is one common way to live with unresolved emotional pain. Broken promises can be deceptive.

Dad said, "We will throw the ball around on Saturday." "I will teach you how to fish." "I will take you to the amusement park." "You can watch a ball game with me."

Mom tried to cover for him and ease the rejection. "Dad is tired. He works hard."

I could say, "He never promised." "He couldn't help it." "It didn't hurt."

This would be self-deception. The attitudes, actions, and words echoed, "I am not that important." "I probably wouldn't learn anyway." "I would mess up." "I would be a bother to Dad much."

I learned not to make promises to my children. I did promise myself that their dad would find a way to be there for them. I want their memories to be of an involved, supportive father.

You might pretend *the injury never happened.* If you admit someone hurt you, you try to believe you took care of it. You attempt to convince yourself that you are over the hurt and it does not bother you anymore. You might want to believe that you already *worked* through it. Not so. Ask yourself, if you worked through the issue, what did you do? If you cannot describe and demonstrate the *work* you did, you most likely buried the issue instead of resolving it.

Time can dull the cutting edge of suffering, but time doesn't heal wounds. Although God works in the process called time, it is He, not time, who heals your hurting heart.

The emotional pain might lose some of its initial intensity, but the wound is still horribly present. When the wound is even slightly touched by a similar circumstance, your soul erupts with excruciating pain that can paralyze you once again. The full emotional intensity of the original hurt reappears and causes you to lash out at whoever happens to be in your path. A relatively small incident in the present taps into a huge reservoir of pain from your past. Your reactive behavior is all out of proportion to the current circumstance. People are accused of making mountains out of molehills. It does not make sense to anyone, not even you.

At a time like this, you might be labeled as a rageaholic or described as having an anger problem. Yet, there is an honest and accurate reason for your explosive behavior. Although such responses are understandable, inappropriate words and actions should not be excused or dismissed. One offense does not excuse another. Your inappropriate behavior is not justified because of a prior incident. Instead of deceiving yourself, find relief from your pain. Then you will be able to stop hurting those around you.

"Self-denial: There is no pain."

Denial says, "The pain is not there." This coping behavior is actually encouraged by the family and friends who say they love you. They accuse you of causing problems when you confront the issue and truly seek reconciliation. They might accuse that you are vengeful and attempting to retaliate.

Some suggest that bringing up the past does no good. "The past is the past, and it cannot be changed," Others advise, "Just pray about it and handle it yourself," or "You are not a very spiritual person if you can't handle this without dragging in others." These folks might really be saying they do not want to deal with the emotional debt they incurred against you. It is easier to blame you or someone else. They do not know how to fix the problem. They do not want to fix the problem. They do not want to try. They want you to leave it (and them) alone. To deal with the debt will cause them uncomfortable feelings, which they want to avoid at all costs.

You might feel restrained or limited in your effort to cancel the debt and resolve your emotional pain. However, while we should be completely responsible and sensitive with our timing, words, and actions, we should never ignore the debt just because someone else does not want to deal with it. Canceling the debt is an act of love. It opens the relationship and brings the possibility of intimacy. If either party chooses to ignore the debt, the relationship might continue, but it will be superficial.

Self-destruction: Pretend the pain was never there.

Some believe that they do not have the right to have emotional pain. They have been taught not to trust their own emotions. One parent said, "You are not hurt. You have nothing to cry about. Stop your crying before I give you something to cry about."

It is self-destructive to *pretend the pain was never there.* Life's experiences might have taught you the false messages that you don't matter or that you are not important. Even though you pretend your pain is not there (and never was), it grows and grows, causing you to choose self-destructive

37

remedies and alternatives for removing it. Obsessive-compulsive behaviors, addictions and/or codependencies might find their way into your life. Alcohol, illegal and/or prescription drugs, spending, gambling, money, sex, dependent or inappropriate relationships, excessive work hours, exercise or other destructive behaviors are ways to escape dealing with your misery. These patterns of behavior do seem to numb the pain for a while by distracting your attention. The problem comes when reality sets in again. You realize that your situation has not changed at all. The troubled relationship you tried to avoid is still troubled. Your heart still aches. You cannot escape your pain by destroying yourself with unhealthy habits. You only make it worse.

Self-delusion: "The hurt is not that bad."

Self-delusion occurs when you try to convince yourself that *the hurt you feel is not that bad*. You can handle it. You can live with it, or at least you think you can. However, you cheat yourself by trying to live your life while minimizing your pain.

One woman shared the common response, "I am fine." She later expressed that *fine* was an acronym for, "Feeling insecure, neurotic, and emotional." She further explained, "Sometimes, when really bad things happen, I ask myself, 'How am I supposed to feel?' I honestly do not feel anything. I suppose that is extreme self-delusion."

My response to her statement surprises some. I suggested that she feel grateful rather than not feeling anything. Traumatic experiences create great pain. If I felt all the pain of the trauma immediately, I could become overwhelmed, possibly leading to a breakdown. Some suggest that emotional numbing is caused by adrenaline; others recognize God's grace sustaining His child. In any event,

I thank the Lord that emotional denial exists. It provides opportunity to exist with the trauma without becoming overwhelmed or paralyzed. Resolving emotions will be addressed later on the journey.

Self-degradation: "I am not worthy to feel my true feelings."

You might not feel worthy to acknowledge or talk about your emotional pain, much less experience healing. Proper self-care and protection are foreign to you and usually make you feel guilty. You might not nurture yourself because you don't feel worthy of affectionate care and attention. Perhaps you do not know how to care for your needs (it is possible that no one ever taught you). When you try, it probably feels very strange to take proper care of yourself. You feel out of your "normal" comfort zone. A new comfort zone needs to be learned.

Unsuccessful attempts to take proper care of you in the past have resulted with more problems. This teaches you not to trust your self-preserving instincts. This, in turn, causes insecurity. You sense a need for control over circumstances and people. You might struggle with anger, tolerate abuse, or continuously withdraw from relationships. These reactions are very different from the healthy, self-nurturing manner God intended for you.

"David encouraged himself in the Lord his God" (1 Samuel 30:6b, KJV).

Conclusion

To know you are a child of the Most High God is essential for spiritual and emotional well-being. You are precious because God loves you. Learn to abide in Christ and trust God as your Provider. He offers you spiritual wholeness and personal health for you to enjoy. Often, the path to healing seems long, hard, and even dreadful. Remember, it is a growing process without a known agenda or time schedule. At times, you might feel that it will never be worth the effort and pain. However, for those who take the pilgrimage, the peace and serenity that is discovered along the way goes beyond what words can communicate.

When you try to pretend you aren't hurting or allow others to convince you to ignore your pain, you actually end up deceiving, betraying, abusing, and denying yourself. The truth is, you *are* hurting. As a result, emotional pressure builds up inside you. The longer the issue remains unresolved, the more the inner pressure builds. At some point, you not only live with the pain, but you are also trying to cope with the pressure. Both the pain and pressure become relentless. As a result, you build walls (usually unconsciously) between yourself and others. You avoid people. You hold grudges. You get angry often and react inappropriately toward people who are not responsible for what you feel inside. You feel tired, exhausted, and worn out physically and emotionally. Life seems to dish out more than you can take. You become sick and tired of feeling sick and tired. At this point, you become desperately aware that you must do something different. But what? Everything you try fails. Every pathway you choose ends up at a dead end. Now what? Forgiveness? "Yeah right!" "I don't think so!" You might not take the journey... yet. I hope you find that you *must*, sooner rather than later.

The fulfilling life you desire is dependent upon your walking down the path of forgiveness.

A Time for Reflection

1. What are coping behaviors?

2. Identify and tell of a coping behavior you have used in the past. What are the words or actions you used? Are you still coping in this way?

3. Describe a situation where you find yourself currently using a coping behavior.

_____

_____

_____

_____

_____

_____

_____

_____

_____

_____

_____

_____

_____

_____

_____

_____

_____

_____

_____

Resisting the Journey

If this is your first exposure to the journey of forgiveness and its process of recovery, you might feel anxious, nervous, or confused. These feelings, mixed with your hurt, can cause you to resist forgiving someone who has wronged you. This confusion and emotional resistance leads to insecurity and fear within. Misunderstanding these emotions has a paralyzing effect. It prevents the necessary actions through which one pursues spiritual health and wholeness. Staying as you are without knowledge of the proper responses will hinder the solution for your emotional pain.

Your view of forgiveness might be colored by past misunderstandings, emotions, and/or rationalizations. The things you learned about forgiveness might be inaccurate. For example, "If you forgive someone, you don't need to discuss the issue with him or her," or, "After forgiving, your mind will be clear of the entire incident." Replacing these false ideas with the correct understanding of forgiveness will enable you to forgive, despite your conflicting feelings. In time, quiet confidence and peace will replace your current negative emotions.

"And the peace of God, which transcends all understanding, will guard your hearts and your minds in Christ Jesus" (Philippians 4:7).

When you understand the stressful feelings and thoughts that attack you and cause you to resist forgiveness, you can gain hope and courage to press on toward healing. Resistance is much easier to overcome when you become aware of the cause. Let's examine the factors that could pressure you: misunderstandings, emotions, and rationalization.

Resistance to Healing Because You Misunderstand Forgiveness

Confusion and fear occur when you misunderstand the true definition of forgiveness. Forgiveness does not mean giving in, giving up, wimping out, admitting defeat, or excusing another's responsibility toward you. We have already established that it certainly does not infer that a person forget the offense. We must replace these wrong definitions with the correct understanding of "canceling the debt." Only when you have an accurate picture of what it means to forgive will you be able to receive the benefit of the "you don't owe me anything" message.

Resistance to Healing Because of Your Emotions

When you begin to acknowledge your deep-rooted hurt, you might fear that forgiving another will bring up the deep pain of the past. Facing those memories seems overwhelming. Escaping the pain is now a major theme in your life. The thought of turning around to deal with these emotions might seem completely ludicrous, repulsive, unreasonable, and impossible. You might feel, "It's just plain nuts, and I am not going to do it!"

Many do not acknowledge or take positive action in response to their need. When they do this, they run the risk of not healing. Spiritual and emotional immaturity can result. Don't let that be you. You can face the pain, and you can overcome it. Once you understand your need for healing and get a glimpse of what life will be like afterward, you will hopefully enter into the journey of forgiveness.

In order to do so successfully, it is important to develop inner strength and courage through your relationship with the Lord. An outward support system of safe family, friends, and perhaps a minister or personal counselor is an asset; each of these is an excellent source to keep you from giving up, giving in, or losing courage. God knows just who you need to help you on your journey. He knows you will need reassurance along the way. Ask Him to place you in the safety of godly counselors and people who will be supportive on your healing journey.

"Where no counsel is, the people fall: but in the multitude of counselors, there is safety" (Proverbs 11:14, KJV).

Resistance to Healing Because of Rationalization

It is easy to talk yourself out of the journey of forgiving the people who hurt you. Confusing thoughts add to your anxious emotions, and before you know it, you cancel the trip of a lifetime. Take courage. Christ is on the side of spiritual and emotional health. Faulty reasoning that causes you to doubt might include thoughts such as, "After it's all said and done, nothing will change anyway," or, "I probably won't do or say it right, and everything will be worse than when I started."

Some drag their feet for other reasons. The offenses hurt, and a natural response is to blame the offender, hold onto resentments, and desire justice. Each party might hold out for his or her own idea of an ideal resolution rather than trust God for His will to be done. Many fear that forgiveness will make them more vulnerable to further injury. Others might feel victimized and long to be absolved. Any doubtful thoughts cause you to feel tossed back and forth between whether to proceed or whether to wait.

"A double minded man is unstable in all his ways" (James 1:8).

Although it is important to wait on God's timing in your life, procrastination is not God's way. God's plan is for you to admit to Him that you are anxious and uncertain of the steps you need to take. After you confess your fears, He wants you to ask Him for what you need to proceed on your journey: strength, courage, boldness, gentleness, or wisdom.[4]

God desires your acknowledgement that He is the source of your strength. Thank Him for being present in your time of trouble and for always hearing and answering your prayers. Finally, the peace of God will guard your heart and mind in Christ Jesus. Anxiety and worry will turn to quietness of soul and peace of mind.[5] Often, it is not rational to forgive, but God did not call us to logic and worldly wisdom. Instead, He has invited us to a higher level of living, loving, and being. He has urged us to live apart from the rest of the world, to change our thoughts so He can change our lives.

"And be not conformed any longer to the pattern of this world, but be transformed by the renewing of your mind" (Romans 12:2a).

If you are to be whole, you must listen to and follow His supernatural call, which beckons you to wholeness. God always calls you to submit to His work in your life through the power of the Holy Spirit. He wants to renew your mind and transform your life. As He replaces your old ways with His new ways, you become spiritually mature. Your thoughts change. Your choices and actions change. Your feelings and emotions change. You become different. You become whole.

There is an inner tendency to avoid conflict. This might be especially true when you address areas you avoided in the past. Don't allow this to prevent you from entering the journey of forgiveness. When you are unsure of the outcome of such a confrontation, it is even more difficult to get started. It is crucial to pinpoint and acknowledge the source of your resistance. Yield your mind and emotions to the control of the Holy Spirit, and press on. Remember, as wonderful as the results might be, it is important to have realistic expectations. Life is not a fairy tale. There will be times when parts of this journey will not be a delightful experience. There will be difficulties.

There are no guarantees of ease throughout the journey; you might temporarily conclude that the trip will not be worth the effort or the risk. Be assured that it will be worth it all. Though the resistance may be great, God is greater. The journey must be taken. It will be worth it. Promise. "Let us not become weary in doing good, for at the proper time we will reap a harvest if we do not give up." (Galatians 6:9 NIVUS)

A Time for Reflection

1. Why do you resist the healing journey of forgiveness?

2. Who might be a good support person for you?

3. What do you typically do when you feel confused?

4. How do you usually deal with strong feelings such as anger?

5. What types of things do you do to avoid conflict?

WE MUST REPENT

Repentance means to turn around and find the other way. Repentance occurs when you accept and act on God's truth. Simply hearing the truth does not ensure acceptance in your heart and mind. You must take action. The evidence of true repentance is seen in how you do things differently. It is like breaking old habits, yet, it is much more than that. Repentance is an inside change that becomes evident externally to those around you. This process involves the work of the Holy Spirit. He transforms you from the inside out. When there is true repentance, your actions will differ because of the inner change of your heart, soul, and mind. False repentance occurs when you try to behave differently on the outside yet still think, feel, believe, and behave the same old way on the inside.

When you truly repent, your responses become different. You begin to notice that your attitudes, words, and actions are not the same as before in the same circumstances. Your thoughts, values, and actions undergo a process of major change. You are growing up in Christ. You are becoming more like Him. (In the next chapter, we will take an in-depth look at your role in this process of becoming more like Christ.) As you grow, you will experience a sense of awe and a feeling of accomplishment and excitement as you realize your refreshingly new response to a difficult situation. In the past, perhaps you exploded, pouted, or reacted with any number of other inappropriate behaviors, but now there is freedom, peace, and power flowing from within you. Repentance does not lead you simply to modify your outward behavior; instead, it guides you to totally put off old practices and put on new actions.[6] This happens as you renew your mind and your heart with the truth of God's Word.[7] It is a complete change from the inside out.

Not only will you see the outward evidence of true repentance, but people around you will see it as well. Be aware that others might not like these changes in you. They felt comfortable with you as you were. If you are different, they too might have to adapt in order to maintain a relationship with you. Change is frequently a difficult adjustment for others, especially if their behavior toward you has been out of line. Since repentance enables you to think and act differently, it also causes you to filter the behavior of others through the truths that have changed your life. In turn, you begin to respond differently to the inappropriate behavior of others. You begin to set boundaries in ways that are firm but loving and kind. Chances are that they are not accustomed to your having boundaries and limits. This might be uncomfortable for you and for them at first, but the adjustment is necessary to build genuine intimacy and closeness with those you love.

A Changed Response to False Messages

This new and unfamiliar way of life will require you to continue to identify and analyze the spoken and unspoken messages you receive from others. In the past, they controlled your thoughts, feelings, and actions. You might recognize any of the following as familiar:

False Messages

There is something wrong with you.

You are the problem, not what happened.

You are no good.

You are not good enough.

It is your fault.

Quit feeling sorry for yourself.

You should have done something to prevent this.

You expect too much.

Get over it.

Stop thinking about it.

Forget the past.

These are false messages that directly conflict with the truth declared about you in God's Word. In Christ you are wonderful and an awesome spirit being of magnificent worth as a person.[8] These negative statements are not the truth. God said so.

If you do not rid your mind of these false messages and replace them with the truth, the same dysfunctional living patterns you have always known will continue to paralyze and cripple your personal growth. Perfectionism, super-responsibility, tunnel vision, or a martyr complex are all evidences that you have believed false messages. The truth never pressures you to live your life in these ways.

Learn to believe the truth. Discover a new way to think. Gain understanding of emotions and behaviors that will move you away from your former dysfunctional comfort zone toward a more godly walk with Christ. As a new thought system begins to emerge, it will also challenge how you look at yourself and others. You discover that in Christ, you do not have to live life pushed to either the liberal or legalistic extreme. You can now live a balanced life in accordance with His grace, mercy, and love.

Acknowledge Your Experience

Another part of the repentance process is to acknowledge the truth of what really happened to you. You experienced pain. Everyone has. Some experience more trauma than others but all of us have experienced some form of emotional pain that has left us feeling distressed, abandoned, and in despair. You do not have to stay in this painful place. You can move forward.

It might be difficult to accept that the one who wounded you may have been violated also. For example, a verbally abusive mother might act out of the pain she received from her own parents. Her current abusiveness is not excused because she herself was hurt as a child. Even though there is no excuse, it is sometimes easier to forgive the verbal abuse of the mother when you are aware of the treatment she experienced in her own childhood. The same holds true with any offender. Forgiveness can be easier when we consider the difficult past of the offender. Let me repeat, being sensitive to the offender's past in no way infers that you should ignore his inappropriate behavior today.

Creator God designed you with an innate desire to be loved and to love others. God intends for this exchange of love between family and friends. You have the privilege and responsibility to love, protect, and provide for each other; but often, the deepest heart wounds come from those whom you expected to love you. Because they loved you, you trusted and believed that because they loved you, their actions would be loving. Even if it was evident to someone else that you were hurt, you might have thought you were loved. Your basic safety was violated, and your soul was left void. All the while, you were thinking, *This is love.* It wasn't. This wounding of your soul created a debt.

Once you recognize that you have a wounded soul, you might spend years blaming the ones who hurt you or incorrectly blaming yourself. Blame has been the natural response of humankind since the Garden of Eden. God demonstrated clearly and completely in Adam and Eve's relationship that forgiveness needed to replace blame. The same is true for you. Debts exist in your relationships, and these debts must either be paid or forgiven. Forgiveness is His choice to cancel the debt of sin and its consequences. It is your choice whether you continue to live holding onto resentment or to walk forward in grace. You can choose to extend to others what God has given to you.[9]

How You Were Hurt

Different types of hurtful behavior or lack of adequate care caused the wounds of your soul. The one who injured you may not truly know he or she hurt you, but your soul is wounded just the same.

Voids

Relationships require nurture. Neglect creates voids. Sometimes the deep emptiness of neglect is dismissed with excuses such as, "I am working to provide for you and buy you nice things." An empty, aching heart would rather have the void filled with the availability and interaction of the person she loves rather than the material gifts. When someone you love gives you "things" without being emotionally available in the relationship, you are left feeling hollow. The gift of things is meaningless without the emotional support, acknowledgement, validation, and love.[10] A listening ear, a tender heart, and gentle words nurture in a much more significant way.

Remember in the opening chapter how Christine's parents treated her? She experienced awful violations of physical and verbal abuse. She also endured something more subtle: the absence (void) of affectionate, nurture, and care from her parents. The emptiness of emotional neglect is less obvious than physical abuse, but it leaves the heart wounded just the same.

Christine shared more of her story with me. She started dating her husband, Joe during her teen years. Two years after they married Joe reminded her of an emotionally neglectful incident that she did not recognize as such at the time it occurred. When Christine was a teenager and dating Joe, she became quite sick with the flu. Severe stomach pain doubled her over. She felt sticky, achy. She cried out in her weakness and pain. She was hoping for something or someone to soothe her and make it all go away. Christine's mother was overwhelmed and had had all she could take. She told Christine to go to her room because the moaning was getting on her nerves.

Sometime later, Joe called to find out what time he should pick up Christine for their date to the local fair. As soon as he found out how sick she was, Joe came right over. He thought she needed soup. There was no soup in the pantry. Joe told his future mother-in-law that he was going to the store to get Christine some soup and asked her permission to heat the soup in her kitchen. It was only at this point that Christine's mom considered that she had turkey broth in the freezer that could be thawed for Christine to eat.

Christine says that even though Joe was never exposed to emotional neglect in his own life, he recognized the situation for what it was. She knows that it would have been easy for him to miss the subtle signs. God opened Joe's eyes to her experience as a teenager and softened his heart toward her. She believes God knew she needed Joe and his family. She is glad that he didn't choose to walk away after seeing the abuse and neglect which were obvious to him.

There are other possible voids. They might take the form of little support and encouragement or the lack of preparation for life. You might think of something not mentioned here but is very real to you. Identify the unfulfilled need and recognize it for what it is. The void must be filled. This is part of the forgiveness journey. You gain the potential to meet the needs of others when your needs are fulfilled. Rather than being neglectful yourself, you change and nurture relationships by meeting legitimate needs.

Physical Violations

The violence of physical abuse is the most obvious to discover. Bruises and fractured bones are easily detected today. There are training requirements in many responsible vocations to note and report indicators of possible physical abuse. There are always emotional injuries when physical abuse occurs. Even if or when the physical injuries heal, the emotional scars need special attention. The healing journey not only addresses the scars but also provides alternative actions. This protects the injured person from further harm. It also provides a new direction to the wounded person so he or she does not become an abuser.

Sexual Abuse

Sexual abuse may be the deepest and most damaging form of abuse because it is such a personal and deeply intimate violation. The violator is often mistaken to be a safe person worthy of trust, causing the betrayal to be genuinely devastating. The physical injury can be horrific. The emotional trauma torments beyond expression and impacts an entire life. When sexual abuse occurs in a religious context, the ramifications are amplified even more. The religious person having a position of responsibility and authority is expected to have a higher moral character and live holy and pure. Ministers are understood to represent God and suggest a greater responsibility to offer care and safety. It is understandable why some transfer blame to God.

Sexual abuse can be falsely justified as acts of love done for the benefit and pleasure of the other person. The violated person may be told, "You enjoyed it." This can be infuriating to those violated. It can also be very confusing if there was some arousal involved. This is abuse! Don't believe the lie! There are many occurrences reported and many more not reported. Healing is possible for the abused. The sexually abused person does not have to stay wounded and broken for life. Continue the journey.

Passing on Your Hurt to Others

To deal with any of these offenses, you learn to cope with life in unhealthy ways, such as playing the role of a martyr. You might become manipulative, depressed, or passive-aggressive. You might try to control others with your aggressive (or passive) anger. Maybe you resorted to obsessive-compulsive behaviors and addictions. Perhaps you maintain a controlled manner but use an intolerant, penetrating tongue to belittle and pass on your criticism and wounds to others.

Very possibly, you did not understand or realize how your actions hurt your relationships. It might be that these hurtful behaviors were included in the kind of "love" you saw demonstrated. Therefore, to you, this is the normal means to love and relate to others, but you must know it is not the only way. This is where and why true repentance must occur in your life. False messages, regardless of their nature, along with abuse and neglect, must be recognized for what they are. Only then can you deal with the damage.

Emotional and spiritual wounds that rip the soul can be camouflaged in the context of sweet words. Until now, you believed these false messages were true and, therefore, you lived emotionally oppressed under their debilitating effect. That is, until now. Now you have gained enough maturity and strength to confront the real issues and truly repent. Remember, true repentance means to turn around, to accept and act on God's truth. This brings you into a new and different way of living. As you apply God's Word, you experience a new way to think and behave. You have a new understanding of your feelings and of God Himself. It is new because it is accurately based upon truth. No more believing the lies of the past. In order to experience this newness of life in Christ, you must submit yourself to God and be renewed in your mind. The transformation you experience will enable you to enjoy the Spirit-filled life that God has designed for you.[11]

A Time for Reflection

1. What false messages have you received?

2. What pattern of thoughts, feelings, and behaviors have you experienced from these false messages?

3. What true realities must become a part of your life?

4. Identify some voids (care, nurture, or skills you did not receive) that are present in your life.

5. Identify some violations (hurt, abuse, betrayals) that are present in your life.

_____

_____

_____

_____

_____

_____

_____

_____

_____

_____

_____

_____

_____

_____

_____

_____

Part Two: Understanding

> The Spirit of the Lord will rest on him the Spirit
> of wisdom and of understanding, the Spirit of
> counsel and of power, the Spirit of knowledge and
> of the fear of the Lord and he will delight in the
> fear of the Lord. He will not judge by what he sees
> with his eyes, or decide by what he hears with his
> ears. (Isaiah 11:2, 3)

As the Holy Spirit reveals the truth to you about your spiritual and emotional pain, may He also give you understanding about what you have experienced and how He wants to heal your hurting heart through the grace of forgiveness. As you come to know Him more intimately, may you understand how your relationship with Him will equip you for your relationships with others. In this, may He give you quick and thorough understanding.

Be a Willing Participant

A preeminent principle in the Bible calls you to be holy as God is holy.[12] Although God made you holy in His sight at the moment of your salvation, there is also a process of growth in which you become holy during your lifetime. This process is called sanctification. Sanctification, the direct result of true repentance, takes place in your daily life as you believe God's Word and depend on scriptural truth to guide your actions. It happens when you do more than just read Bible verses. You believe them. You act upon them. The Bible is relevant to your circumstances. You are transformed as you trust Him and obey what He reveals in His Word.

As you begin to see your Christian life in a different light, being a Christian becomes an adventure. Life has more meaning. When you are sanctified by the Truth, the Holy Spirit's power transforms your natural reactions to people and situations into supernatural responses to those same people and situations.

For instance, when you are saved, God sees you as holy just as He sees Christ as holy because you are now "in Christ."[13] Just because you are a Christian does not mean you automatically differ in the way you respond to people and situations. You change progressively by applying biblical truth in a series of events spread over the course of your lifetime. Applying the Word of God in real-life situations changes your thinking and, ultimately, your feelings. You were born with a sinful nature. Even when you are born again spiritually, your mind, emotions, and will might still be in subjection to your former way of relating. The old way is based upon what you have personally learned and experienced in your life up to the point of your salvation. The beauty of becoming a Christian is in the supernatural and transforming power of the Holy Spirit who now lives in you. It is He who does the work, not you.

You can know the truth because Jesus is the Truth. When you know Him personally you will believe truth; and respond to it, you will become free from old behaviors you thought would always rule your life. You do not have to behave in certain ways because that's just the way you are. While you do have personal responsibility in this process of sanctification, you need His love, mercy, grace, and forgiveness. You have no power of own to overcome the power of sin that is still present in our lives. The Scriptures make it clear that sanctification is the work of God. This process involves the change of our own self, which includes our thinking, our emotions, and our will. Your only responsibility is to submit, yield, surrender, and humble yourself. If you believe in God's truth for salvation, you shortchange yourself to live in any other way than believing and acting upon His truth moment by moment and situation by situation.

Most likely, there are times when you, as a child of God, erroneously believe that what you want in life is actually better than what God chooses for you. This is a common belief stemming from a lack of understanding and trust in God's ways, His Word, and His promises. In order to be healed and freed from pain, it is essential that you accept by faith that God is good, God is love, and His ways are the solution. His thoughts are higher than yours.[14] Submitting to His will and following His teaching will produce the best results in every situation.

In His model prayer, Jesus clearly speaks to us about forgiveness. He teaches us to forgive others as the Father forgives us.[15] Even if we do not like it, this command is clearly written in Scripture for our own good as well as those who offended us. When you refuse to forgive, not only are you centered on your own pain but you are unable to see the pain God experiences when you are unforgiving of others. Fellowship with God is broken. You do not seek forgiveness for yourself and, therefore, cannot extend forgiveness to others. In other words, your hurting, hardened heart will actually prevent your heart from being softened to see your own sin and seek God's forgiveness. If you are presently living in a state of unforgiveness toward another person, you need to experience God's forgiveness in your own life. Allow these feelings you have pull you toward God and His great forgiveness rather than push you away from others.

Personal Privilege

To forgive and to be forgiven is an amazing act of God's grace showing Christlikeness in you. What an opportunity! The privilege is yours, as an act of your own free will. You can discover the forgiveness that is available for you personally. When God reveals a lack of forgiveness in your life, it is time for action. Ask God to search your heart for the need of forgiveness, whether you need to accept it or extend it or both.[16] Then obey so that you may enjoy the full potential that the Christian life has to offer.

Personal Prosperity

God's plan is to prosper you, not to harm you.[17] True forgiveness enables you to enjoy His prosperity on a daily basis. This is not the materialistic, pleasure-seeking, instantly gratifying affluence that dominates our culture. Rather, it is His inner spiritual joy and serenity that satisfies the longings of your heart, soul, and mind. The comfort heals your deep wounds and provides the courage to continue the journey to wholeness. This prosperity does not only fix a temporal problem; it has eternal benefits, providing a crown of life in the world to come.[18]

This journey of forgiveness requires the unique grace, courage, strength, and confidence through faith that is available to you in Christ. His love compels you to forgive. With Him, in Him, and through Him, you are able to uncover your tender wounds and clean them in the spirit of His love and compassion. Forgiveness requires bold love. "Bold love is courageously setting aside our personal agenda to move humbly into the world of others with their well-being in view, willing to risk further pain in our souls, in order to be an aroma of life to some and an aroma of death to others."[19]

A Time for Reflection

1. In what areas do you need to experience God's forgiveness in your life?

2. In what relationships do you need to grant forgiveness to someone else?

_____

_____

_____

_____

_____

_____

_____

_____

_____

_____

_____

_____

_____

_____

_____

_____

_____

_____

_____

_____

_____

Recognizing Your Unmet Needs

Do you know of a wonderful marriage characterized by mutual love and respect, a marriage where there is both diversity and equality and you can say, "This couple is really doing it right"? Are they effective in raising their children to enjoy their marriage? Better yet, will these children raise children to do the same? How often have you seen families enjoying the multi-generational success of warm, intimate relationships marked by love and godliness? These people enjoy being together, doing things together, and pursuing individual and joint goals. The key word here is *enjoy*. There is kindness and tenderness in words and actions toward each other. There is emotional support and physical intimacy. Grace and forgiveness are the norm. The ability to resolve differences is common. These traits characterize mature godly relationships. Perhaps you do not see this very often or not at all. Sometimes these characteristics are only superficial. However, if you have seen genuine love between two people, you have an example you can follow to build your own healthy relationships.

Needs

If you haven't seen or experienced a healthy family life, you might not even know that you have spiritual, emotional, and physical needs that should have been met in your family relationships when you were growing up.[20]

Perhaps you are just coming to terms with the fact that your needs were never met in childhood.

Such a pain is difficult to understand and hard to accept. But it is part of your journey. Let your pain lead you to depend upon Christ. Cast your burden upon Him. This is what He wants you to do.

God intended for your spiritual, emotional, and physical needs to be met in the context of healthy family relationships. When these basic needs are not filled, the resulting damage is often as intense as that of verbal, physical, or sexual abuse.

God demonstrated the human heart's basic need for acceptance, affection, and approval in the parable of the prodigal son.[21] When this wayward son came to his senses and returned home, his father accepted him without condition, greeted him with warm love and affection, and demonstrated his approval with an open celebration.

If you didn't receive unconditional acceptance, nurturing affection, and appropriate celebrated approval early in your life, this very well could be the cause for your pain today. A critical step in the journey toward forgiveness is to recognize that God intended you to receive these blessings of unconditional love from your parents. Though uncommon, these are the true norms God intended.

After you recognize God's intended standards, determine if they were met. This is critical because until you know the needs, you won't be able to determine if they have been realized in your life. You might not recognize the deficiency and, therefore, the hurt caused from these voids. As senseless as it sounds, you might be hurting and not even know it. You might be numb to the pain. Until you become aware and feel the hurt, you cannot recognize the debt. Until you recognize the debt, you cannot forgive; until you forgive, you cannot be healed; until you are healed, you cannot enjoy living the life of fulfillment God has planned for you.

"Hope deferred makes the heart sick, but a longing fulfilled is a tree of life" (Proverbs 13:12).

By now, you are probably beginning to understand the voids and violations in your life. These can be described as debts.

Debts

What is a debt? What does it look like? How does it feel? The natural eye cannot see the spiritual or emotional debt directly. It is easier to see the after effect of the offense than the actual wound. For example, if an angry father kicked his child, you might see the bruises or broken bones. These observable, physical injuries heal and might not even leave a scar. But that same offense can cause a major wound on the heart of that victimized child. Though it remains unseen to others, this emotional and spiritual wound constantly aches within the child. The child's father might not even remember the physical attack, especially if drugs or alcohol are involved. He might never even ask for the child's forgiveness. Perhaps no one considered the role of the older, lying sister who instigated the rage of the father. This horrible incident leaves deep injuries that affect the relationship between the child and his father, his older sister, his absent mother, and his future wife and children. This hurting child will become a hurting teenager, and before long, he will be a hurting adult unless there is forgiveness somewhere along his journey. Though physical wounds heal with time and medical attention, internal wounds require spiritual attention and forgiveness for healing to take place. If, at any point, he desires to build safe, genuine, and intimate relationships, forgiveness must first take place. Reconciliation, restoration, and intimacy are only possible after bitterness, rage and anger, brawling and slander, along with every form of malice are put away and replaced with God's loving-kindness, tenderheartedness, and forgiving spirit.[22]

Debt results from an offense. Offenses might be verbal, emotional, spiritual, physical, or sexual in nature. They leave the offended party injured in some way. Appendix A has a brief outline of physical, verbal, and emotional abuse. It is intended to help you recognize its various forms, relieve your doubt, and confirm your thoughts about abuse. The ability to identify mistreatment provides the strength, courage, and confidence essential for the journey. Sometimes simultaneous injuries are referred to as psychological issues. The reality of the injury and the pain and confusion that crush your wounded soul matter more to you than their labels. Relief from the torment might be the only thing of concern.

Our Heavenly Father is deeply concerned about you. When injuries occur, some commonly blame God. "Why did you let this happen?" The real truth is that God cares for you very much and is brokenhearted over your pain.[23] Jesus came to bind up the brokenhearted.[24] God could have arranged for those things to be prevented. He could have stopped the offender from saying what he said or doing what he did. But He didn't. Perhaps you might feel like there were two offenders: the person who hurt you and God, who stood by and let it happen. What you question is that if God loves me, why did He let this bad thing happen to me? Even though it hurts, God wants you to see yourself, the offender, and the situation from His perspective. His ways are greater than yours.[25] God uses affliction to shape your life and mold your character to make you more like Christ. His hands are shaping you through the painful experiences you have suffered as you depend on Him for understanding and healing. God also uses hurt to teach you about Himself. It was evil, not God, that influenced the offender to hurt you. God is all-powerful, all-loving and just; He can use the effect of evil in your life. In the midst of your pain, God is sovereign and in control. He does not shield you, but He will be with you and deliver you through it.[26] He will be faithful to heal and grow you in character and in spirit.[27]

The Catastrophic Damage

It is possible that you are genuinely ignorant of the wounds in your soul. Maybe you grew up in an atmosphere of neglect, abuse, drugs, or alcohol. Your family might have had divorce, unmarried or missing parents, step-parents and step-siblings, half-siblings, or a loss through death. Your parents might have been caught in the web of workaholism, materialism, money, or the lack of spiritual direction. If so, God did not intend for you to have this kind of family. Sometimes, families use religion and church activities to justify neglect and irresponsibility and then call it sacrifice for God. What is of primary importance with God is a personal relationship with Jesus Christ. It is not to be involved in every ministry and church activity. Your relationship with your spouse, children, and family is also paramount. God instituted the family before He established the church. With balance, it is possible for parents to love, nurture, and discipline their children in the Lord.

A critical point in the forgiveness journey is to realize that God created you with basic needs that might have never been met ever. Understand what your needs are, and learn how they can be met within the boundaries of a healthy relationship with God and others. It is difficult to know your needs and understand how they can be met if you have never observed people relating to each other in the way God intends. You might think that what you have experienced is what God intended, even if you experienced neglect or abuse. The media continually keeps the horror of neglect and abuse before our eyes and ears. Our society is desensitized to it and its far-reaching effects. Because it is so common, it seems that families are supposed to be dysfunctional and abusive. We see so many stories that we have just accepted that this is the way of life in our nation and world. People raised in dysfunctional homes might think, *I had good parents. I came from a good family.* But nothing can be further from the truth. God never intended families to be so destructive.

The Collateral Damage

One way to recognize your unmet needs is by paying attention to inappropriate behaviors. This can indicate that you have covered up emotional pain that desperately needs to be addressed and resolved. Emotional damage that has been suppressed and not healed is often referred to as unresolved emotional issues.

Specific inappropriate behaviors that are indicators of this include but are not limited to depression, anxiety, panic, acts of anger and rage, reliance on prescription drugs, addiction to illegal drugs, overeating, bingeing, purging, spending money, or gambling. In addition, some people "act out" in relationships or activities. If these patterns are present, and if you realize and acknowledge them, they will likely point you to an underlying wound that causes you pain and impacts your life on a regular basis.

In some cases, a drug problem might show that someone is trying to medicate an emotional or spiritual wound. Medical doctors consistently report that a large percentage of their patients have unresolved emotional pain causing physical symptoms. Generally, these patients are baffled or offended with this diagnosis. They prefer medication to deal with the physical symptoms rather than receive counsel to deal with the spiritual and emotional causes. Remember, physical medicines do not heal spiritual or emotional illnesses. Physical pain requires physical medication. Emotional pain is in your soul, not your physical body. Only the healing balm of the Great Physician, Jesus Christ, can heal spiritual and emotional pain and restore your soul.[28]

Although prescription drugs might help for a short time, they only numb the pain; they do not heal the wound. The problem here is you will not seek healing for the cause of the emotional pain if you cannot feel the pain. Even if you lessen it, the temptation is to accept the pain when it should never be tolerated.

Most acting-out behaviors, including using prescription or illegal drugs to mask emotional pain, are usually done unconsciously. Using this destructive method hurts you (the original victim) and everyone around you as you pass the hurt from person to person and from generation to generation.

Hurt people hurt other people. Although you are suffering, your offensive actions toward others cannot be excused. You are still fully responsible for your actions, attitudes, and behaviors. This accountability helps break the cycle of hurtful reactions. When you become aware of this cycle, you begin to understand that when you harm others, often, it is because you are hurting deep within your own heart.

When others stop tolerating your inappropriate behavior, they become a catalyst for you to take your journey more seriously. When someone else cares enough about you and their relationship with you to confront and rebuke your inappropriate behaviors, they create the greatest opportunity to change if you choose to do so. They are revealing the need to stop the destructive reactions and behaviors for your own good and for the good of the relationship. At the same time, you don't need to wait for others to hold you accountable. They might help you, but ultimately, the change must come from your acknowledgement, repentance, and reliance upon God. The changes must come from within.

You might be genuinely unaware of your emotional pain.[29] Even when a family is aware, it is surprisingly common for them not to address these hurtful behaviors. They would rather avoid than confront a person or an issue. Sometimes, even when family members are aware of the pain, they are genuinely unaware of its destructive results or they feel helpless and hopeless, not knowing what to do.

More Collateral Damage

If you have not received acceptance, affection, and approval[30] in your past, you are handicapped in developing intimate relationships in the present. Fears, whatever the source, prevent you from getting close to your spouse and others. You might lack effective communication skills, feel worthless and undeserving, and experience insecurities that paralyze you from establishing healthy and successful relationships. Past failed relationships and rejection might also add to your resistance to intimacy and avoidance of vulnerability. Problems in your personal and professional relationships leave you (and others) feeling frustrated, distant, empty, and confused.

Knowing and understanding your unmet emotional and spiritual needs helps you admit that you are hurting. You might also have to admit that you were abused. Often, those who have been mistreated feel they are victims for life. It is unfair to be a victim. Most likely, you had no choice in the matter. You do not have to remain a victim. You only continue this role by holding on to hurtful words and actions. You can choose to be free from the victim mentality. Forgive the original person who hurt you. You do not have to be their victim forever. Remember, you are not responsible for what others have done, even if it was done to you. You might have been shamed and humiliated. You can and must stop the dreadful reality of thinking you are still a victim. Continue the journey so you can experience the healing freedom and joy God intended for *you*!

Before you can find relief, you must come to terms with the fact that you are hurting, and you must desire to know and understand why. Up until this point, all you might realize is that disturbing feelings have gripped your very being. You are most aware of them when you are quiet and still. In order to avoid the pain, you might try to keep yourself busy. You might sleep, work, exercise, clean, shop, or even do things in the church to keep these feelings buried. But as soon as it's time to wake up or end your task, distressing feelings invade you again. So, you find another activity to keep your mind occupied. God desires to use your personality, gifts, talents, and skills. He has given them to you to accomplish great and meaningful things that glorify Him, benefit others, and bring fulfillment to your heart and soul. But you cannot do this until you are still long enough to know Him[31] and allow Him to restore your wounded soul.[32]

To recognize your unmet needs is not easy. It might seem much simpler to ignore and avoid your pain, but this will keep you from truly knowing, loving, and enjoying your relationship with God and others. Continue on this journey of forgiveness without distraction. Recognize your unmet needs now rather than later. May God strengthen you with might by the power of His Holy Spirit in your inner man.[33]

A Time for Reflection

1. What are the basic needs of children as they grow up?

2. Identify the basic needs of children that were not met in your childhood.

3. Identify the personal violations you have experienced.

4. List appropriate opportunities or privileges you did not experience as a child.

5. How have you passed these voids and violations on to others?

_____

_____

_____

_____

_____

_____

_____

_____

_____

_____

_____

_____

_____

_____

_____

A Time for Recollection

To recognize unmet needs might not be easy. It is often painful. When you realize there are needs that are not met, you are well into the journey. Facing the needs while managing your current state of affairs along with meeting the demands of others might be very hard. It might seem overwhelming or even impossible. It is not. Your emotions might scream, "Yes it is!" You might feel desperate. Some choose fight while others choose flight.

So, exactly what is recollection all about, and how do you do it? It is that time when you uncover[34] and bring to mind those situations and people who left tremendous emotional debts in your heart and mind. It is a time to organize your thoughts and feelings about these injuries in your life so you can do the necessary work to forgive.

Your Support Program

I strongly encourage having good emotional support available to you as you begin your reflection and recollection. A faithful companion on the journey at this time is priceless. He or she might be able to help manage the emotions and circumstances. The next leg of the journey will be much more stable when good support is involved. I believe there are four components to a fully complete support program:

> ### Four Components
>
> 1. Biblical counsel
>
> 2. Emotional support
>
> 3. Self education
>
> 4. Sharing your story

Biblical Counsel

It is not wise to explore the past alone. A complete support program will include biblical counsel. To have a counselor coach you along this journey to help decide actions and timing will keep you safe in many ways.[35]

A pastor who is available and understands the forgiveness journey may be used by God to support and counsel you. However, because God has created and designed each of us with unique gifts, maybe he is more gifted in a ministry other than support and counseling. This one-on-one work with people is a delicate discipleship ministry. If your pastor does not counsel with you, it does not mean that your pastor is indifferent to your personal concerns; it might just mean that his strengths and calling fall in other areas. Be discerning. Don't become discouraged or bitter if your minister cannot be your emotional support and counselor for this kind of growth and healing. Possibly, an older woman or man who is also a believer, a family member, or a deacon could counsel and disciple you. Your church should be able to refer you to a Christian counselor in your area who counsels according to biblical principles. [36] Find someone who has patience to support you on the journey. Let the Spirit of God, not impatience, lead you.

Emotional Support

Choose your support people carefully. Support can come in two forms: advice and comfort. In the beginning, it may or may not be wise to depend on your spouse for emotional support. It is very easy for a mate to give well-meaning but less-than-appropriate advice. The level of spiritual and emotional intimacy you have in your marriage will help determine whether you need emotional support outside your marriage.

Good support people will be able to listen, and listen well. They will not crumble when you feel like you are falling apart. They will not react, criticize, judge, condemn, or take advantage of you when you are down. Those who assist will not tell you what you have to do. Instead, they will help you think about your choices and encourage you to walk in wisdom and in faith.

To be a support person is very demanding and time consuming. It takes a special kind of mature Christian to support you. Often, it requires someone who has personally taken this healing journey already. Choose people who are emotionally present and provide comfort without judgment and condemnation.

When you are considering possible confidants, *never, ever* consider one of your children. You might be their encourager, but they should always be your child.

Self Education

It is crucial to begin your forgiveness journey with as much good information as possible. Possibly, you have been introduced to some of these concepts for the first time and they seem very unsettling and confusing. Try to determine the truth. Learn as much as you can about the healing journey, and consider it in light of the Scriptures. Often, God exposes sojourners to many resources. Take full advantage of the opportunities for growth and healing that come your way.

It is also important to begin to piece your own story together. Try to remember as best you can what happened to you. When did it happen? How did it happen? What was the setting for what happened? Who was involved? What role did each person play? To collect what you remember is important to determine the significance of the debt and lead you toward forgiveness. This process becomes valuable when you begin to examine and consider the above questions deeply.

Share Your Story

To share your story is important. At first, this might seem impossible; the pain is often huge and consuming. The shame and humiliation can be crippling. Some try not to think about it; they find the memories haunting. In time and with great courage, you can proceed.

There are many appropriate ways to share your story. Sharing with the Heavenly Father is crucial to receiving His healing. Prayer is an opportunity to discuss these things in a helpful and most surprising way. Some get angry with God. Others accuse Him. Many weep. God is God. He is able, willing, and eager to hear from you. God already knows all your history and pain. He wants to be your comforter. He is in the business of healing emotional and spiritual pain, and He desires to restore your soul. Seek Him early. Tell Him how bad you hurt. Ask Him to heal you.[37] Today is the day of salvation from spiritual and emotional pain.

When sharing your story with others, it is important to know and speak the truth about what has happened. In the beginning, you might only be able to talk about your pain. God will provide others to help carry your heavy burden by listening to you. Share your story by seeking out those whom you can trust to keep your story confidential. God has spiritually gifted many people with mercy, to come alongside and provide compassion to those who are hurting. He wants them to encourage and help build you up in the Lord. Be as open as possible. As you continue to heal and grow, the way you talk about your injury and pain will take on new shape. You will be able to give evidence of God's healing work in your life and, in doing so, provide encouragement, support, and blessings for someone else.

My Story

I will share a story from my own life to illustrate this portion of the journey.

In many ways, it was a typical Saturday afternoon. In many ways, it wasn't. Mom left my sister, Beth, and me with Dad while she went to grocery shop with a neighbor. It was not typical for Dad to care for us in Mom's absence, which is one reason why she did not leave until early afternoon. She prepared our lunch before leaving so Dad would not have to feed us. It was not typical for her to be gone for so long. She usually shopped at the corner grocery rather than go to the next town. Getting away for over an hour with her neighbor friend was an enjoyment for her.

I was eight years old. Dad was watching weekend sports, drinking beer, and snacking on Planter's peanuts. He watched television in the master bedroom with the shades closed so the sun's glare wouldn't interfere with his view. This was typical.

He was irritated with the responsibility to care for his children. Saturday was his day to recover from the week. In that way, this day was no different.

My sister Beth was eleven. Not feeling well, she was in her room down the hall, and I was in mine, until I went into her room to play. Beth's room was across the hall from the master bedroom. As I went into her room, I could hear the television through the closed door. Dad was watching his Saturday afternoon sports. *Typical,* I thought.

Much to my surprise, Beth did not care to play. She became very angry, screamed at me, and chased me from her room. I shrugged and went back to my own room, disappointed that my sister did not want me around. Oh well.

When I heard a commotion in the hallway and came out of my room to see what was happening, Dad yelled at me, "Leave your sister alone!" I was in total shock. Beth was telling Dad that I came into her room and spit on her. I couldn't believe that my Goody Two-Shoes sister, whom I admired so much, was lying about me.

She turned to me and repeated the accusation, "You came into my room and spit on me."

In amazement and with extreme feelings of disbelief and powerlessness, I said, "I did not."

"Yes, you did," she insisted.

"Leave her alone," my dad yelled. Then Dad kicked me like a football.

I flew through the air down the hallway, hit the wall, and landed hard on the floor.

This was not a typical Saturday afternoon.

I do not remember much after that except Dad and Beth returned to their rooms to occupy themselves with their former activities. I went to my room also, preoccupied with what just happened to me. I experienced minor pain in my right shoulder. However, what I felt on the inside was far from minor. Crying alone in my room, my heart throbbed. I was in total shock that my sister lied about me and my dad physically harmed me. I lost all respect for Beth that Saturday afternoon. Previously, she had been my hero. Now, I was angry, bitter, and full of rage toward her. That Saturday afternoon, Beth became emotionally and spiritually indebted to me in ways I would only understand as I grew older.

I know these things are real and they happened to me. I remember them. What did it all mean to me when it happened? What did it mean later? How was I hurt? What things did I start believing about myself as a result of this incident? This part of recollecting is called understanding, knowing what the facts mean.

As I remembered this incident in my life, I grew to understand that because of what happened, I was lonely on the inside. Loneliness was the worst part for me. I felt very alone, disrespected, and unappreciated. The betrayal of my sister made me feel like other people didn't believe in me. In my eight-year-old heart, I felt all alone. I was the victim of lies.

As I grew older, I could not trust my sister to be honest or fair. I realized that my mom would not always be there to protect me and I could not count on my dad to parent or lead our family appropriately. I also began to believe I looked ugly on the inside and the outside. Those around me criticized my physical features. They often teased me about my skinny body, eyeglasses, buckteeth, and freckles. These negative beliefs significantly affected my life. I felt helpless and powerless to convince people that I was not ugly inside and out and found ways of coping with my hurt that were contrary to God's will.

What do you understand and know about the pain in your life? Understanding comes from God. He wants you to ask Him to reveal the truth so you understand the impact of the hurtful events in your life. Most importantly, He wants to set you free from the bondage of what you have believed about yourself and Him that are not true. His desire is to fill you with knowledge of the truth about who He really is and who you are in Christ.[38] The truth will set you free. Seek Him now.[39]

Once you know the facts and understand what they mean, you can begin to walk in wisdom toward spiritual growth and maturity. It is wise to obey Christ's teachings on forgiveness. In each step of this journey, He will give you wisdom to make choices and take appropriate action. Wisdom is insight and skillful living in the circumstances of life that helps you to enjoy life.

Quiet Time to Think

With a support program in place, you are ready to reflect and recollect. To gather the facts and educate yourself, take an inventory of the hurts in your life. It is best to set aside quiet time to think and remember your past. Record your thoughts and feelings by making categories of hurtful events that best help you determine the debts you need to forgive. You might choose to gather and record memories one relationship at a time. Or you might collect memories according to the different types of wounds you have experienced. It is not important whether you start at the beginning or end, front or back, top or the bottom. If you tend to be a perfectionist and want to be sure that you get it right, remember, there is no right way. Whatever method seems most productive is the best way for you. The important thing is that you begin and then continue the journey in the strength and support God gives moment by moment. There is no timetable for the journey.

Your Forgiveness Journal

So what about you? Why are you hurting? If you were asked to research and record the spiritual, emotional, verbal, physical, or sexual offenses in your life, where would you start? Who comes to mind? What situations were most painful to you? When were you left to hurt while others continued on with life as usual? How did you cope then? How did you cope later? How are you coping now?

When you begin to consider questions like these, it is helpful to create a forgiveness journal to record your thoughts and feelings. Journaling during your forgiveness journey (did you ever notice the similarity between journey and journaling?) can prove to be an emotional experience. You begin to recall events you have not thought about for a long time. Don't be surprised if tears result from the things you remember and feel. Do not let tears keep you from recording your thoughts and feelings. They are part of God's healing work. It is all right to be angry over sin, to cry over what has hurt you, and to grieve over what has been lost through the years. God uses tears to help cleanse the hurt from your heart as you journal or share your experiences.

Writing in your journal is an opportunity to clarify your thoughts, express your long-pent-up feelings, and create a place to begin understanding yourself and your past. At first, the writing might be difficult. Collecting memories takes time, space, and energy. Allow yourself to daydream, to start opening the doors of the past hurt. Do not worry if you cannot remember certain times of your life. Work with what you remember, and if more memories are important, God will give them to you at the right time. In real life, not every single offense needs to be addressed individually. Forgotten offences are forgotten. Love covers many offenses.[40]

Some offenses cannot be overlooked and must be addressed. Offenses can cause injury. They hurt. It can be helpful to consider some of the different forms of abuse. Abuse can be physical, verbal, emotional, or sexual, among others (see Appendix A). Abusers might try to convince the abused that their abuse is not really abuse. But it is. It is very important to recognize abuse and the damage caused by abuse for what it is. This understanding is important to continue the journey of healing and forgiveness.

If you are one who struggles to express yourself, there is a "Glossary of Feelings" words at the end of this book to help you express your feelings. Remember, your journal is just for you. It's private and doesn't need to be shared with anyone else. No one needs to approve of it.

The following questions might help you open up emotionally. You may answer these questions for each hurtful offense or for each person involved in each offense.

These questions are also outlined in Appendix B.

Q1. What was the incident? (A topic sentence.)

Q2. What do I remember about the incident? (Tell the full story.)

Q3. Who hurt me?

Q4. How was I hurt?

Q5. How did that hurt impact my life in the past?

Q6. How does that hurt impact my life now?

Q7. How might that hurt impact my life in the future?

To help you understand how to answer these questions for yourself, let me answer them for you according to my own story.

Q1: What was the incident? My sister lied, and my dad kicked me.

Q2: What do I remember about the incident? I wanted to play, and my sister did not. My mom was not home. My sister lied that I spit on her. My dad kicked me down the hall.

Q3: Who hurt me? (To acknowledge who was responsible is not the same as blaming someone. Blame is saying someone else is responsible for my actions. It is evidenced in statements like these: "He had no right to do so and so," "She shouldn't have done that," "You were wrong to do that to me.") In my story, to say that my sister lied and my dad kicked me down the hall is to acknowledge responsibility, not assign blame.

Q4: How was I hurt? My dad hurt me physically. My sister betrayed me. Because of their actions, I felt unimportant, disregarded, rejected, and unloved. I felt betrayed by my sister. I felt insecure, abandoned, defenseless, and helpless in my mother's absence.

Q5: How has that hurt impacted my life in the past? The day of the incident, I was physically sore. My shoulder hurt. Emotionally, I felt betrayed, disrespected, shocked, all alone, mistrusted, and punished without understanding why. Spiritually, I could not trust my sister to be honest or fair, nor could I count on my dad to parent or lead our family. I felt unprotected because my mother was not there. Socially, I was afraid to tell her what happened. I did not think she would believe me. After all, it would be my dad and sister's word against mine. She would side with them, and I would not be heard. A possible tongue-lashing from my mother echoed in my mind. "I can't leave you at all. I can't count on you to behave."

As the years progressed I felt unsafe in relationships. It became difficult to trust. I feared rejection. I struggled to develop relationships yet longed to feel safe and loved. Insecurity and loneliness became the backdrop of my life.

Q6: How does that hurt impact my life now? (The healing journey is taken in adulthood. The following response is from my life when I began the process.) There are countless ways the past impacts my life today. My adolescent struggles continued into adulthood. I convinced myself that other people thought I was an ugly or mean person and felt helpless and powerless to convince them otherwise. In my heart, I knew I was not a mean person, and I genuinely loved others but could not figure out how to get them to believe this was true. I feared I would be unjustly punished for the wrong actions and behaviors of others. There are many ways the past challenges my life today. How the past impacts my life today is significantly influenced by my daily choices.

Q7: How might that hurt impact my life in the future? I can continue to live my life out of the old pain and patterns of the past, or I can learn to live in grace. History does not change. People in my life today will most likely repeat behaviors that remind me of my past. These actions can trigger me to overreact to mild circumstances. This causes harm because I pass on the hurt to others. That is why we say, "Hurt people hurt people." Sometimes I am painfully aware of the way history triggers current behaviors. Sometimes I am very unaware. The people around me might be conscious long before I notice. It is very important for me to be open, humble, and teachable to those closest to me. They will help minimize hurting others around me.

Now, before you begin to collect and record your own thoughts and feelings, consciously come to Christ with your heavy burden. When you do, God will meet you where you are. The Holy Spirit will walk with you to reveal those things you personally need to remember and forgive. He will comfort you, understand you, and care for you as only He can.

What if you have already done this work? Even now, you might realize that you have already made this pilgrimage in your own life. If your wounds were genuinely healed in the past, enjoy your growth and prosperity today.

It could be that you are called by God to help someone else bear his or her heavy burden. Please be patient with

their pain. Some of the most precious growth and healing take place when a person remembers and expresses
the emotional trauma he or she experienced in the past.
It takes enormous courage and strength to express and
share deep emotional pain. A special grace appears, and a
unique intimate bond occurs in this very sacred moment.
It is holy ground. Treat it with the utmost respect
and confidentiality.

Forgive as You Go

Whether you did this work of forgiveness years ago
or if you are now getting involved for the first time, your
pilgrimage toward healing and wholeness is a process that
continues throughout your lifetime. The future will hold
more hurtful experiences that will require you to forgive
if you are to continue to walk in spiritual and emotional
freedom. As you mature, you will realize that when issues
surface, learning to forgive in the moment is a valuable
tool of daily life.

Like a child, begin to forgive as you go. Children state
the debt by telling it like it is. They tell who and what
hurt them. They cry their tears and get on with whatever
they are doing. They forgive. We need to return to that
childlike behavior. The alternative is a life of unforgiveness
characterized by resentment, bitterness, anger, and rage
(among other miserable things). Childlike forgiveness is a
far better and easier lifestyle than the alternative.

A Word to Encourage You If You Are Just Beginning This Journey

Begin your forgiveness journal and continue on this journey as you are ready. Jesus Christ is dwelling in your heart by faith and is willing and able to carry your burden. He is within to empower and strengthen you. He is ahead to lead you. He is alongside to support, comfort, and walk with you. But He is not behind, trying to force you.

Chapter Seven

A Time for Reflection

1. Make a list of potential support people.

2. Approach three of them and discuss with each the possibility of being an emotional support person for you.

3. Prepare a forgiveness journal.

4. List some of the different offenses in your life that need to be dealt with on your forgiveness journey.

5. List some people whom you need to forgive.

6. How have the offenses against you impacted your life? Share this with a support person.

7. If you have already been on this journey, consider someone you might support who is ready to begin.

_____

_____

_____

_____

_____

_____

_____

_____

_____

_____

PART THREE: WISDOM

"If any of you lacks wisdom, he should ask God,
who gives generously to all without finding fault,
and it will be given to him" (James 1:5).

May you find wisdom in your time of suffering. May
you believe and act upon all truth the Holy Spirit reveals
to you. May you rely on Jesus, our Messiah, to continue
the journey. Do not give up. God wants you to experience
complete growth. May you be quick and skillful to know,
understand, and apply what God is teaching you in your
time of suffering.

Cancel the Debt

Consecrate Your Heart So Love Can Rule

After you have researched and recorded the spiritual and emotional debts others owe you, the next step in your forgiveness journey is to cancel these debts.

Emotions

When you are ready to cancel the debts within your heart, it is crucial to be aware of strong or angry feelings. Feelings act as motivators for your actions. If you are careless, they might be used to destroy you and others. It is destructive when feelings of anger cause you to blame or punish someone rather than forgive. If you are wise, they can be motivational for your healing and growth. The wise alternative is to realize, identify, and accept these valid feelings of anger and then turn them into positive actions to release your offender from the debt he owes you.

The energy produced by your angry feelings has a source. Sometimes emotions, such as anger, are secondary emotions.

When Anger Is a Secondary Emotion

When you feel angry, it is usually a secondary emotion. The primary emotions include fear, frustration, or pain.

Possibly fear of an accident from being cut off by another vehicle causes an angry reaction toward another driver. Frustration from waiting in a long line might cause an angry attitude toward your energetic child waiting with you. The hurt and pain from stubbing your toe on a chair can cause you to be angry with the chair. It's silly but true.

It is very important to know and understand why you are angry in the first place. What fear, frustration, or hurtful pain is at the root of your anger? God wants you to examine yourself to find the true source of the problem in a manner which benefits all. His direction for you is to forgive, not avenge or take matters into your own hands to settle the score. He judges with mercy and righteousness (something we are unequipped to do in our human nature); vengeance belongs to Him.[41]

"Refrain from anger and turn from wrath; do not fret it leads only to evil. For evil men will be cut off, but those who hope in the Lord will inherit the land" (Psalm 37:8-9).

We have seen that blame and revenge are not God's way to deal with an offender. Neither should your primary focus be on how to deal with the pain. Your responsibility is to forgive. Your spiritual and emotional health, which goes hand in hand, depends on your willingness to do so.

Spiritual Wounds

The ideal process of "canceling the debt" includes sharing your injuries with the offender.[42] Remember, injuries include all kinds of wounds. They might be physical, emotional, psychological, or sexual. If physical abuse took place, physical damage occurred. If verbal or emotional abuse took place, there was psychological or emotional damage. No matter what type of abuse took place, and regardless of whether the violation was physical, emotional, psychological, or sexual, you were definitely violated spiritually. All injuries have a spiritual aspect to them. God's Word teaches that people should be loved and nurtured. Anything contrary to this is a violation of His spiritual law. It is much easier to see wounded flesh than a wounded spirit. However your spirit is offended rather than loved, wounds are created in your soul.

We see physical injuries with the natural eye. Emotional and psychological injuries become apparent when they are verbalized. To merely vent your pain will not satisfy your spiritual need. That is why this part of the journey blends the following four phases:

Four Phases

1. Consecrate Your Heart

2. Construct Safe Boundaries

3. Cancel the Debt

4. Confront the Offense

This chapter considers "Consecrate Your Heart." The other phases are covered in the following chapters.

God has called us to respond to His greatest commandment, to love Him and to love others as He has loved us.[43] It is easy to love the lovable. Yet it is much more of a challenge for us to love the unlovable. Apart from the power of God's grace, it is incomprehensible, even absurd and impossible to love our enemies. Yet, His grace can empower you to love and to do good to those who mistreat you.[44] Jesus lives His life in you through the power of the Holy Spirit. He enables you to love and forgive. You do not have to create your own forgiveness, love, or acceptance toward another. These attributes belong to God, and they are available to you.

The Lord works all things together for your good. Search out the gems God has hidden in your trials. Learn to believe God's Word and renew your mind. The renewed mind develops the ability to replace old thoughts with the truth of Scripture. His Spirit will empower and enable you.[45] It is not complicated to move a mountain. But it requires a lot of effort, time, and resources. *Although this truly is simple, it is extremely difficult.* When you understand God's parameters for relationships and receive His grace, you learn to love the offender and mountains move.[46]

A Time for Reflection

1. Identify the feelings from an offense of your past.

2. Determine which underlying emotions of fear, frustration, or pain that might also be present.

3. Write a prayer purposing to not sin in your anger.

4. Write a prayer that demonstrates your intent to forgive your perpetrator.

_____

_____

_____

_____

_____

_____

_____

_____

_____

_____

_____

_____

_____

_____

_____

_____

_____

_____

_____

Construct Safe Boundaries

Safe boundaries stop further injury. They will protect and prevent further violations from occurring. A boundary also establishes a safe atmosphere and nurtures mutual love and respect. The average person does not intentionally put himself in harm's way. Hurt people want the pain to stop. They do not want to place themselves in a relationship in which they will continue to be victimized. There needs to be a zero-tolerance policy of abuse.

Holiness is an example of separation of that which is holy from that which is not holy. A boundary is the dividing line that separates. In personal relationships, a boundary separates the injured person from further abuse.

Many boundary limitations can separate a victim from the perpetrator. To establish a boundary, a person might limit communication, separate to a different room, hang up the phone, delete unheard or unread messages, or use time and distance. It can be a spoken statement to the offender to explain what will and will not be allowed in the relationship.

Ideally, the offender will recognize the offense and cooperate with the healing journey. When this happens, it eases the journey and creates hope. The old, hurtful relationship must no longer be tolerated. A new relationship includes mutual care, safety, respect, and consideration. This takes time to develop and requires healing and growth. It might be very difficult to learn this new way to live. Often, there are setbacks and times of discouragement. Do not let discouragement cause you to faint.[47] Make no mistake about it— the new relationship is worth working for. To endure or tolerate abuse is never worth it. By God's grace, determining this new way to relate is doable; very difficult, but very doable.

Unfortunately, there are situations when the offender will not cooperate. It is very important to establish sturdy boundaries to enforce the zero-tolerance rule. This should be done with love and grace. Even when the boundary is placed with loving kindness, it might be resisted or even challenged aggressively. The offender might use harsh words, false accusations, physical abuse, or other hurtful reactions. If you find yourself in this situation, do not allow any form of intimidation or fear to paralyze you. You might feel overwhelmed, but you do not have to let those emotions stop you from the journey. Find a way to manage the emotions and continue. Find help to protect yourself with godly boundaries. Learn to establish and maintain the zero-tolerance boundary with strength, conviction, love, and grace. Do not allow abuse any more. God says you are precious and need to guard your heart.[48] Protect it no matter what.

In their book series on boundaries, Drs. Henry Cloud and John Townsend show how boundaries impact all areas of our lives. Physical boundaries help us determine who we will allow to touch us, in what way, and under what circumstances. Mental boundaries give us the freedom to have our thoughts and opinions. Emotional boundaries help us deal with our emotions and disengage from harmful, manipulative emotions of others. Spiritual boundaries help us distinguish God's will from ours and give us renewed awe for our Creator.[49]

The boundaries we set with others might not be a guaranteed protection from abuse, just as restraining orders are not always respected or effective. Clear boundaries address the sinful behaviors that will not be tolerated and establish a safe and acceptable framework in which to resume a relationship. They need to be discussed and enforced with the other person. You may or may not need to go back and clarify the past. It is always necessary to deal with issues and offenses as they arise in the present.

A Relationship of Balance

Elizabeth and Laura were best friends for years. At a certain point, Laura began to notice that the friendship was one-sided. It seemed that she always listened to Elizabeth talk about what happened in her daily life. Elizabeth rarely inquired about Laura's well-being or daily struggles. Throughout their friendship, this was the norm.

In order to feel good about herself in the relationship, Laura needed to listen. Elizabeth talked for the same reason. But when Laura began to grow spiritually and emotionally, she realized that a truly fulfilling relationship allowed time for both friends to listen and share. Laura began to share, but Elizabeth did not begin to listen. This hurt Laura deeply. She made several attempts to tell Elizabeth how important it was that she share her life also. Elizabeth still was not willing to listen and even became offended with Laura's new behavior. Even though Laura forgave and even asked Elizabeth for forgiveness, Laura's newly established boundary of sharing her thoughts and feelings was not immediately respected. Respect might be very hard to gain, but in a mutual relationship, it is essential.

Many care enough to learn how to develop a mutual relationship. They find the new personal dynamic valuable and worthwhile. The boundary setter often becomes a precious gift and friend for life. My life experience has shown that most people learn and grow. Others never understand. There are a few incorrigible people who will just not change. Abused people must recognize the dangerous people, avoid them, and keep them behind firm boundaries. Thankfully, there are not many of these folks. But do not be quick to write off all difficult people; many appear to be resistant at first but begin to appreciate proper boundaries with time. This slow and difficult process requires patience and persistence. Remember the beginning of your journey. Look what you are doing now. Surprising? You are making progress. Maybe slow, but that is okay. Keep on keeping on. You will be thankful in the end.

When there is emotional, verbal, or psychological abuse, it is common for an abuser to criticize or insult others. The aggressor can be extremely cruel yet not understand the severity of the problem. The lack of understanding might be due to the norms of the life experienced in the aggressor's childhood. Criticism and sarcasm are often used to satisfy selfish desires or cover up insecurity. A boundary should be established by refusing to continue a conversation with someone who is angry and manipulative. If the verbal abuse is severe and a long-standing behavior pattern is in place, it will take a long time to break old patterns and master new ones. In situations like this, you need courage, determination, and strength to establish and maintain healthy boundaries.

When you set boundaries and reestablish a relationship with an offender, the relationship changes. At first, it feels awkward to be together. You are not accustomed to relating to each other in this new way yet. Do not expect your new relationship to cause you to forget the injuries of the past.

There might be physical scars that will always remind you of the injury. Emotional and spiritual scars bring back memories of the painful past. *When you remember the pain the debt caused, you must also remember the commitment you made when you forgave.* You have cancelled the debt in order to create an atmosphere in which your renewed relationship can grow and become meaningful.

It is crucial to note that some relationships will never lend themselves to restoration. For example, it is possible to biblically forgive severe criminal acts. This frees your emotional and spiritual pain. At the same time, it is not wise to establish or reestablish a relationship with a murderer, rapist, or dangerous offender. Severe criminal acts can be biblically forgiven, but there are occasions, such as murder or rape, when it may not be wise to establish or reestablish a relationship.

Boundaries Regarding Sexual Abuse

We frequently hear of sexual abuse or molestation. Let us be sure we understand the extent of sexual abuse. Sexual abuse is:

> Any activity, verbal, visual, or physical, engaged in, without consent, which may be emotionally or physically harmful and which exploits one person in order to meet another person's sexual or emotional needs. The person does not consent if he or she cannot reasonably choose or consent or refuse because of age, circumstances, level of understanding, and dependency or relationship to the offender.[50]

(See Appendix A.)

For example, it is always abuse when any superior or authority figure is involved with a child or subordinate. Sexual abuse cuts across all lines and distinctions. Naively, some families do not recognize the deep horror and atrocity of sexual abuse. In denial, some might minimize its effects. Others might express outrage or even banish the offended and/or the offender from their family circles. However, please recognize that sexual abuse is a criminal activity and must be treated as such. All sexual abuse must be reported to the appropriate authorities.

Let us illustrate how to set a boundary when someone has experienced sexual abuse. After the legal issues are addressed, it is necessary to protect the victim from ever letting a situation arise where he or she could be vulnerable to the perpetrator and violation again. A further boundary might be necessary to protect from the emotional impact. Most likely, the injured party will not want to be in the presence of the offender. After the issues of responsibility, restitution, and restoration are addressed, there might be a time to consider reconciliation.

The healing journey of forgiveness challenges you to confront the offender. It is very important to have good sturdy boundaries in place before you confront someone. The response could be volatile and vicious. When good boundaries are present, you can withstand the reactions of a perpetrator without any further damage. You can learn to interact with an offender, still be very safe, and benefit regardless of the reaction.

Chapter 10 explains the purpose and goal of confrontation and prepares you to accomplish the work of forgiveness.

A Time for Reflection

1. What principles will guide you to establish safe boundaries in order to protect yourself from further injuries or harm?

2. Write out a statement of how you would communicate a boundary to an offender.

CANCELLATION

There comes a time when you must "cancel the debt." Forgiveness is an activity of God. When one chooses to forgive, he participates in a genuine spiritual activity.

Every person sins and therefore incurs a sin debt. This debt must be paid. God has determined that He will accept the payment of Jesus who voluntarily became our substitute by His death. The sin debt is satisfied this way. When a person recognizes his sin and calls on the name of the Lord, God rescues him from the consequences of his sin. The offender is pardoned; he is debt free, forgiven. The debt no longer exists. God determines the appropriate consequences in the life of the offender. It is no longer a concern for you, the offended. In like manner, when I forgive, I consider my offender to be debt-free.

Forgiveness recognizes the offense and the consequences. The one who offers forgiveness is able to discuss the offense and the debt to be forgiven. He or she trusts God with healing, justice, and possible reconciliation. Forgiveness has nothing to do with punishment of the offender to make him or her feel bad. Of course, godly sorrow with repentance is a desired response so the offender also experiences spiritual growth.[51] The purpose of the confrontation is not only to recognize the offense; it also announces your complete cancellation of the debt. Do not address the offender until you are ready to forgive. When you forgive, you give up all efforts to hold the other person responsible for the debt. You no longer want to punish the offender or see him or her suffer. You give up anger, resentment, and a desire to be vindicated. This is not complicated, but it is the most difficult part. Like a child, you express what hurt you, cry the tears, consider the debt paid in full, and move on in life.

The declaration of forgiveness obligates the forgiver to act as though the offense never occurred. There is a practical outworking of forgiveness. Forgiveness might be lived out as shown in the Five Commitments of Forgiveness also listed in Appendix C.

The Five Commitments of Forgiveness

1. I will not think about this incident *without also remembering the grace and forgiveness I extended to the offender.*

2. I will not bring this incident up and use it against the offender.

3. I will not talk to others about this incident *unless talking about it will be an opportunity to glorify God for His healing work in my life or the life of others.*

4. I will not allow this incident to stand between us or hinder our personal relationship. *In fact, I will seek to use the grace present as a catalyst for a more godly relationship.*

5. *I will seek to understand the offender and show compassion.*[52]

There is a progression through these commitments. It begins in the life of the forgiver. Next, it addresses the relationship with the offender. Then, it explains how the offense will be discussed with others. Fourth, it removes barriers and encourages the relationship. The last commitment is a challenge of understanding and godliness.

This journey is not for the faint of heart. Do not be discouraged. Remember the tremendous benefits of forgiveness. This leg of the journey is built on all the previous elements. The injury must be acknowledged and the debt determined. The events must be communicated in an appropriate manner with safe boundaries. Reconciliation may or may not be possible. This will be discussed later.

Question One About Cancellation

There are several difficult circumstances that interfere with this process. For example, what do you do if the offender is deceased? Obviously, it is impossible to confront face to face. Instead, write a letter to the offender. God knows this and understands. This enables you to express the effect of the offense in your life. Share the truth, and then explain and cancel the debt. This process will help bring healing and freedom.

There might be even greater healing if you read the letter aloud at the offender's grave. It would be proper to take your emotional support person along. It will be more meaningful if your support person not only has a close relationship with you but who also knew the offender and aware of the offense. Possibly he or she may have also been affected by the offense in some way.

Question Two

If you are in a twelve-step recovery program, you likely have a sponsor. A good sponsor is trained to support you;

however, he probably did not personally know you before the recovery program, does not know your offender, and was not aware of the offense until you shared it with him. He was not your brother who witnessed the awful episode in your home as a teenager. She is not your sister who grew up in the same household and suffered her own emotional trauma over the years. Your sponsor is not a colleague who experienced the same overbearing rule of an ungodly superior. It is rare if a sponsor or anyone unfamiliar with your circumstances can adequately support you. Who then would be a good choice to aid you in your journey? The closer your relationship with your support person, the more significance you experience on your journey. It is one thing if a new friend knows what happened and supports you in your pain; it is quite another if your brother or sister stands by to encourage and help.

Question Three

What happens when the offender does not apologize? Most people believe they need to hear the other person say he is sorry in order for forgiveness to be complete. But fortunately, this is not true. Forgiveness is to cancel the debt without expecting an apology. In his sermon, "Forgetting to Remember, Remembering to Forget," pastor and evangelist Dr. Ike Reighard summarized how to cancel the debt like this:

> To cancel the debt is a matter of the will. You make a conscious choice to release the offender from any claims you have against him. This includes claims like having to hear him say he's sorry, or having to hear her say she was wrong or that she did you

wrong. Cancelling the debt means coming to the point where you're willing to forgive your offender and move on with your life by releasing all claims. To cancel the debt is to choose a right relationship with God, yourself, and the other person over your personal rights.[53]

Break Free from the Spiritual Bondage

Up until this point, the wound has kept you and the offender spiritually bound to each other as a debtor is bound to a lender or as a slave is bound to a master. This is because the wound created a spiritual unpaid debt. Very likely, every time you think of this person, you feel resentment and anxiety. This is emotional torment. This is spiritual bondage that can only be broken if you free the other person of what he owes you and forgive the debt.[54]

Freedom comes when you declare the debt canceled in full. When you pardon the debtor, and he goes on without owing you anything, you begin to experience emotional and spiritual healing. You are finally free.

Forgiveness is also a process. Remember when you began to recall the hurtful situations and injuries in your life. Most likely, you have more than one wound caused by different people at unrelated times in your life. You must confront each individual and cancel each debt separately. For example, Mom doesn't owe Dad's debt. Each must be held accountable for his or her own. This might overwhelm you at first, but the further you travel on your journey, the more confident you will become. This is God's way to heal the emotional and spiritual pain in your life. Though you have suffered many wounds, the resolution of the most severe injuries lessens the effect of the remaining ones.

When there has been a very intense hurt in your life, even small incidents or offenses that touch the wound feel big. Just like when you bump a paper cut. It hurts. For example, even the untimely end of someone's visit might bring back painful feelings of rejection and abandonment.

After cancellation takes place, your previous unexplained, uncontrolled emotions begin to change because God uses forgiveness to heal your pain. When you hurt, your emotions can be up and down like a roller coaster, but when you have healthy emotions, you become more stable. At first, you struggle to think, feel, and behave in new ways. Yield your old ways to the control of the Holy Spirit. Continue to trust God and believe His Word. Believe that He is living in you and responds to your circumstances. This is the new Spirit-filled life that begins to emerge from within you. When you sow the right seeds, you enjoy a rich harvest.[55] It will become more and more evident to you and others. When the Lord heals your hurts, you are healed.[56] It is a common occurrence that a person who once raged at the smallest events like a child demanding attention now calmly responds to the circumstances of life. Halleluiah! Praise God! Chapter 13 discusses the resurrected life in more detail. As you "cancel the debt" internally, you prepare to confront the offender.

A Time for Reflection

1. Express in writing your intention to forgive the debt.

2. Write about how the offenses you have suffered have impacted your life then and now. Share this with a support person. The more you write and share, the more freedom you experience.

_____

_____

_____

_____

_____

_____

_____

_____

_____

_____

_____

_____

_____

_____

_____

_____

_____

_____

_____

_____

_____

_____

Confront the Offense

The most difficult step of the journey is to confront the offender. Past experiences might have taught you to avoid confrontation at all costs. This person hurt you. When you did something that he or she did not like, you paid for it. Perhaps you did nothing at all but paid for it anyway. It is normal to expect that the violator has not changed and maybe never will. This is one of the most hopeless and helpless feelings in life. Even if the violator has changed, he might have caused so much hurt that you would rather never see him again, much less confront him. This is even more stressful if the person is still a real threat or danger to you.

"Can I just think about it?"

"Can I just write it down?"

"Can I just tell someone?"

"Can I just tell you about it?"

"Can I just write the letter?"

"Can I just send a letter?"

"What about a phone call?"

Yes. Yes. Yes. Yes. Yes. Yes. Yes.

You may do as much or as little as you desire. You can do nothing at all, but it will not accomplish the full process of forgiveness. Start small. Practice safe disclosure before you expose the deep wounds of your soul. To journal might be a safe way to begin. Even the process of writing can bring back dark memories that overwhelm you. Yet recording hurtful situations helps you heal and empowers you to share with safe people. It builds confidence. Perhaps one day you will be able to share your story with strangers. God will use your hurt to help others as he did in my life.

The degree to which you confront the issue is directly proportionate to your personal healing. You choose. The greater the confrontation, the more you will experience healing. The greatest growth occurs when you confront the offender directly. Though this might seem unlikely or even impossible now, your attitude will change as you ask God to show you His way.

You might be far from finished with all of the confrontations and cancellations of your pilgrimage. There is no rush. It is best not to react impulsively. I hope that you have already enjoyed some healing. Some feel better because they have received encouragement, reassurance, and confirmation. They realize they have legitimate concerns and are not traveling alone on the journey. Be encouraged. In time, you will progress.

Why Confront?

It is very common to want to suppress hurtful events of the past. Situations that caused you emotional pain are very difficult to revisit, much less discuss. Yet, you really cannot forget. You might ask, "Why should I go see *him*? Why should I make contact with *her*? Why talk about *it*?" Your reluctance to communicate with the offender is common. However, the sacred Scriptures teach clearly that the road to recovery involves confrontation.[57] A clear understanding of the reasons for and benefits of confrontation can help you do what seems impossible.

A simple physical injury, such as biting, hurts the flesh just as a spiritual injury like gossip hurts the soul.[58] A physical wound needs direct attention for healing, as does your spiritual or emotional wound.

When spiritual boundaries are transgressed, the spirit is wounded. Just as the flesh must be sewn back together for the proper physical healing, so loving confrontation restores the spiritual boundary and heals the spirit.

You might resist confrontation for various reasons. You could be accused of making a mountain out of a mole-hill. You could be misunderstood, and the offender might dismiss the incident. Neither is true. Remember, you are to acknowledge the violation, not tolerate or accept it. You will make this clear when you reestablish the spiritual boundary. To set limits and boundaries enables you to regain the personal integrity that had been ripped away by the offense. You are responsible to speak the truth in love to your offender.[59]

Personal integrity has to do with being whole and complete on the inside. It is being pure about life and clear about what you expect in relationships. It is restoring your emotional state as it was before you were hurt, neglected, or abused. It is reestablishing your belief that others should treat you as God intends them to treat you.

Spiritual healing takes place when the violator is confronted and the spiritual boundary is reestablished. The fullest healing is possible only when a confrontation takes place. This seems to go against the philosophy of man but truly is the mind of Christ. Just as a sincere prayer for salvation changes a person's eternal destiny, so obedience to the biblical command to confront an offender brings you healing.

The Confronter's Confrontation

To confront is difficult. To confront in a godly manner might seem harder, yet to go to the offender without the spirit of love makes matters much worse. A carnal confrontation is a reaction to someone else's reaction. We tend to express ourselves with anger and sarcasm. More offense and injury is likely to occur. To confront in a godly manner can be a wonderful experience. Speak the truth in strong, bold love[60] that is balanced with grace and mercy, kindness and meekness.[61] The soft answer turns away wrath.[62] We are called to rise above the evil so that we might receive the blessing.[63]

The Offender's Response

Even a biblical confrontation can bring an unwelcome response. You might find yourself worried or fearful about the violator's reaction. Although it is never easy to share your injuries with the offender, it is much less difficult if he or she has changed. However, these desired changes are rare.

Therefore, it is very helpful to properly prepare for the possible responses of the offender during the confrontation. Prepare emotionally and spiritually for the worst while you pray for the best. Expect the probability of an undesired response. Perhaps the offender will accuse you of being self-righteous; he might belittle your honest efforts to resolve the conflict. He might try to violate you even more with his anger. Worse yet, he could deny everything. These responses will be difficult to manage. No matter how the offender responds to your genuine efforts, the Holy Spirit will allow you to possess a peacefulness you might have never known in the past.

Your ability to forgive the offender is not dependent upon how he responds to you. You are not responsible for his or her response. In fact, the reaction of the violator is irrelevant. The purpose of the confrontation is not to obtain a favorable reply but to bring the offense to light and hold the violator fully responsible for all the damage he caused by his violation. This will enable you to clear the account, cancel the debt, and reestablish your spiritual boundary. Again, your healing is not dependent on his or her response. Be strong. Be courageous in the Lord.[64]

What Others Say

Some believe to confront your offender is selfish. On the contrary, it is self-preserving. However, even more, it is an act of love to God[65] and for the offender. This is because confrontation and boundary-setting direct the offender's attention to his violation or sin. To be open and honest with the offender with kind intentions is a way to acknowledge the offense and how it felt for you. It also gives the violator the opportunity to express godly sorrow and truly repent.

When he acknowledges the violation with sorrow over his shortcomings, he humbles himself in the sight of the Lord. This person will also receive healing from the Lord that lifts him up completely.[66] Confrontation will most likely not feel comfortable for you or the offender.

Just as a loving father challenges the decisions and actions of a wayward son, you also express the love of God when you confront an offender. It is an act of love for his good.

Your well-being is of great concern to God. When your thoughts and feelings are consumed with pain from what you have experienced, you are not free to focus on the things God has for you. You are in a weakened state emotionally and spiritually. It is possible to remain there until confrontation takes place. In order to gain the strength you need, here are several suggestions that will help you prepare for your confrontation.

Anticipate

It is very helpful to anticipate the offender's responses. Forethought removes some surprises and gives you more sure footing. You might not be able to anticipate the actual response, but preparing for it will help. You will be better prepared for what actually takes place.

Practice

I strongly suggest you practice your confrontation first. You can journal, write letters, which will not be mailed, or role-play with your support person. If you can write it, and say it to a support person, your confidence will be strengthened for the real encounter.

One-On-One

Scripture teaches that confrontation should be done one-on-one first. If the offender listens to you, then you have "gained."

"If your brother sins against you, *go and show him his fault*, just between the two of you. If he listens to you, you have won your brother over" (Matthew 18:15, emphasis mine).

If you confront the violator, but the abuse continues, you might choose to take someone along for a second attempt. Since it is advisable not to put yourself at risk of being violated further or weakened emotionally, the presence of your support person would be a wise choice. There is no scriptural directive or additional benefit in doing it alone after the first time. Remember that your support person is not someone who will team up with you against the offender but rather will lovingly support you and help maintain accountability on behalf of both parties.

Circumstances

Choose the right place for the personal confrontation. Find a neutral and safe location. Often, a public setting such as a restaurant, can be very effective.

The right time is also a serious consideration. What is going on in the life of the person who offended you? Did he recently have surgery? Did she just experience the death of a close family member? Be sensitive to his or her circumstances as well as your own. There is no time schedule in the healing journey. The earlier the healing takes place, the sooner the relief. Healing will occur with the confrontation, but there is no rush. Neither you nor your support person should push through this part of the journey. When you are ready, it will be obvious to all concerned. It's best to practice and plan and pray so you have the courage and energy to proceed. Remember, there is no "right" time for a confrontation. The right time is the time you choose and commit to confront. You might not feel healed or any better at this point. You might even feel let down. It is a step of faith and obedience to confront your offender. Pray for strength and courage. Grow to the point where you "just do it."

A Special Word Regarding Parents

When you forgive the offender, he or she experiences relief from guilt. As you mature in your own life, you realize the impact of childhood voids and violations. You also see that people's best efforts fall short and cause unintended damage to others. Therefore, you must learn to forgive your parents and accept them for who they are.

Sometimes you doubt you could confront your aging parents and cancel their debts because you think it would be unloving, mean, or insensitive. Yet, the very opposite is true. It could be the most compassionate thing you could ever do. For example, you might understand now for the first time under what conditions your parents grew up.

You might begin to realize that your parents loved you and did their best at that time. You begin to understand how and why everything happened as it did.

If you share the offenses of your parents, their first reaction might be very harsh. As discussed earlier, they might deny, accuse, or blame in the beginning. It is common to see that as time goes by, parents who have been confronted begin to act differently. Sometimes they begin to give you respect. Almost always, they will back up to some degree and be less hurtful. Sometimes they will give small indications of willingness to try to work on a godly relationship with you. When these small efforts are "fanned" as coals from a fire, a miraculous relationship can be created over time. I have heard many testimonies of warmth growing out of these embers. Try it. You might be surprised.

Understanding your parent helps you know how the offense happened in the first place. Understanding is important and helpful. This does not mean, however, that you should minimize what happened. But if you know how and why it happened, it is easier to make peace with the past.

As the adult child, you might fear that you will hurt your parents, break their hearts, or even be responsible for their death if you lovingly confronted them. But this is far from the truth. You actually have the power to give each of your parents enormous freedom and relief from the burden of guilt each carries. Encourage your parents to celebrate forgiveness and enjoy a precious new relationship with you.

Consider the possibility that your parents might be carrying guilt because of their painful awareness of their shortcomings toward you. Your parents might ask, "What can I do about it now?" Nothing. "How can we pay the debt?" They can't. They can seek forgiveness, and you can forgive. That is what forgiveness is all about. And only Jesus's death can pay such a debt.

When you move through the confrontation and cancellation phases with your parents, you break down walls of guilt and resentment that have been in place for years. It feels wonderful to tear them down. And once forgiveness occurs in this way, the wound heals, and a wonderful and unique adult relationship often appears and develops. You are both freed from the past and can celebrate the present.

For example, many dads have spent most of their time working long hours to provide for their families. To their way of thinking, they fulfilled their responsibility and therefore took little initiative to care for and parent their children. Perhaps you are an adult child who longed for a relationship with a hard-working father. You searched in the wrong places for this love and participated in the wrong things to demand attention. Please remember that you are always responsible for your own choices and actions, but to understand the desire behind your decisions helps repair the damage. If you explain your longing for a relationship through confrontation, both you and your father can begin to learn how to create a healthy, loving relationship. Don't hesitate. Go for it. Create it. Enjoy it.

During a trauma, it seems impossible to believe that any good could come from what you are experiencing, but Scripture teaches that all things work together for our good.[67] When you spend time considering the big picture, you will be able to see the gems that come from the horrible past. *You can learn to thank God for His gems of blessing hidden among the path of your sorrow and suffering.*

We are called believers, but we walk in unbelief much of the time. Look closely. Decide to believe. God's Word is truth. He will use the awful thing you experienced for your good and His glory.

A Time for Reflection

1. Identify and describe a particular offense or personal violation you experienced and are willing to bring to the forgiveness journey.

2. Express your spiritual wounds.

3. Write out a confrontation statement to your perpetrator. Read it aloud to your support person.

4. Identify the possible reactions you might expect from the offender.

5. What accusations might you receive from others when you confront the offender?

6. Record how the offenses against you have impacted your life. Share this with a support person.

7. Write about how a particular offense affected your life when it happened and how it affects your life now. Share this with a support person.

8. Identify gems you have discovered during the forgiveness journey.

9. Write a letter to each of your parents expressing an offense, the debt, and your forgiveness to them.

10. Plan, and go and confront your offender.

_____

_____

_____

_____

Your Response to the Offender: Now and Later

Forgiveness is possible and necessary regardless of the violator's response or attitude. He might or might not acknowledge and accept responsibility for the hurt. The pathway to healing and recovery is not dependent on his response. But when there is cooperation, it helps to ease the pain.

Now

What is the difference between the offender who acknowledges his offense with remorse and desires forgiveness and the offender who is unresponsive, denies the offense, or even blames you? It is not dependent on the offender's response.[68] When one studies Mathew 18 with the whole of Scripture regarding forgiveness, this becomes clear. Forgiveness or "canceling the debt" in your heart is not the same as reconciliation. Reconciliation is the final goal, but it is not forgiveness. The awareness of this distinction helps to clarify forgiveness with realistic expectations. At the same time, it is much easier to work on forgiveness with the offender who accepts responsibility for his actions than one who does not.

God's forgiveness is comprehensive. Once the sinner's debt is cancelled through forgiveness, it is permanent. The debt can never be paid again because it no longer exists. This is not fair; it is grace. The Lord is gracious and merciful. How does this happen? Why is it possible? Because

God the Father acknowledged the full scope of sin and completely resolved the debt with all its eternal consequences. This was accomplished when Christ paid our debt through His death on the cross. In a similar way, when you acknowledge an offense and do the complete work of forgiveness necessary in your relationships, there will no longer be a debt. You cannot forgive again and again because there is no debt. Once it is cancelled, it is gone forever. You will likely remember serious offenses many times. Discipline yourself to choose to remember differently. To continue to remember the offense and hash it out over and over again becomes your sin. Then you are walking in unforgiveness, and this fosters and nurtures a root of bitterness within your heart.

Forgiveness Means Action

Forgiveness calls for action. Your responsibility is to recognize that God already provided payment for the offense against you and choose to allow it to satisfy the debt. Allow His sacrifice, pain, and selflessness to wash over you and heal your pain so your forgiveness can wash over your offender. This frees you both from the bondage that binds you together in pain.

This does not mean the debt never occurred, nor does it mean there was no damage. If anything, the act of canceling the debt recognizes the injury and its damage. Then forgiveness occurs, Jesus pays the debt (not the offender), and you cancel it. God's sacrificial gift provides healing.

In one sense, the debt might seem to be erased without payment at all. For example, when physical harm occurs, the responsible party cannot physically heal the injury. Even though a skilled surgeon can stretch skin and sew a wound back together, only the healing power of God causes the flesh to grow together and leave only a scar. If there was financial loss, payment might be insufficient or incomplete. Only God can bring the spiritual and emotional healing you desire. Despite the appearance of the circumstances, Jesus Christ has made the payment. The payment is applied in your relationships when God is the actual active agent of forgiveness. The application of this payment, the "canceling of the debt" of an offense, is the powerful activity of forgiveness. Just as large sums of money are transferred from one bank account to another, the transaction of forgiveness is powerful.

Later

There is a wonderful result of genuine forgiveness. Just like the debt, your previous unhealthy, emotional reactions to the offender and the offense are gone permanently. You become spiritually and emotionally free. For perhaps the first time, you become able to respond and interact in a Christlike manner to people. This is also true for the offender.

When You Remember the Hurt

Every time you remember an offense, discover additional injury, or recognize further debt after you have forgiven, *you must also choose* to remember the activity of forgiveness as a completed transaction forever. This needs to be learned, understood, and practiced repeatedly. Choosing to remember correctly might be one of the most challenging concepts to accept and master, but this is the only way to enjoy the fruits of forgiveness. Whenever you remember the offense, decide at that moment to remember the grace of forgiveness. This will help you experience blessing. To remember the incident along with the grace and forgiveness you've extended to the offender means you will not bring up this incident to use it against the offender. There is no place for vengeance and forgiveness to reside together. Forgiveness trusts God to remedy the offense. It also means that any discussion about the incident will only bring recognition to God for His healing work or bring benefit and help others. It will in no way harm the offender. The grace of forgiveness will help build a new and more godly relationship. In addition, it will eventually bring a genuine understanding and sincere compassion for him (see Appendix C: The Five Commitments of Forgiveness.)

It is natural for your emotions to swirl at times. Emotions can be powerful. They do not determine your moral standing and do not need to determine your actions or control your choices. You can make the right decisions even while experiencing intense emotions before, during, and after the process. Your spiritual decision to forgive is what is true, real, and based on the cross of Christ. It will last forever. When you remember the event with God's grace and mercy, forgiveness becomes a positive memory of grace. You must not consider a forgiven offense a debt. You made the decision to forgive. You have removed the debt by its roots. It no longer exists. Grace does.

Let's say, for example, that you forgave your friend for hurtful words. Biblical forgiveness means you acknowledged what your friend said. You told him how his words hurt you. You cried your legitimate tears and, in genuine love, extended your forgiveness. Three weeks later, if you remember those same hurtful words, most likely you will not experience the same degree of pain as before you forgave. Now is the time to yield your emotions and thoughts to the control of the Holy Spirit. You have already obeyed the direction of Scripture to forgive. Remember the offense, the pain, *and* the grace of forgiveness. Ask God to continue to relieve your pain. Thank Him for His healing work in your life. Thank Him for faith to believe, strength to carry on, and courage to obey.[69] Then go about your daily routine. Trust and believe in the peace of God to guard your heart and mind through your relationship with Jesus Christ. Focus on truth, justice, virtue, and things that are lovely and praiseworthy. It will take time, but what you will begin to experience will go beyond your ability to understand.[70]

Is forgiveness a one-time transaction or an ongoing process? It can be argued that since Christ died once and for all to pay the sin debt of all mankind, then you too can, by one act, forgive your perpetrator of all he or she has done to you. Because God is all-knowing, He is able to see man's entire sin debt in advance with accuracy and accept Jesus's payment in full.

Unfortunately, few know or understand all the damage that took place with the offense, or the extent of the damage that occurred from the violations. You will need to take an inventory of the damage caused by the offense, in order to be more prepared to reckon the account of the sin debt.[71]

The total indebtedness of the offender, as a result of the offense, might not be discernable to you all at once. This depends on the particular offense and the time it takes for the full extent of the damage to be exposed in your life. For example, if a child is abused and does not understand the abuse until his teen years, he will only be able to determine the damage that has affected his life up until that point. This is called primary or catastrophic damage.

Initially, you forgive the offender for all you know and can foresee as a result of the offense. As the child matures, he might discover additional effects later in life, during marriage, or when raising his own children. This is referred to as collateral damage. Forgiveness has the power to continue to erase and eventually eliminate the effects of the offense. If you are faithful to affirm that you have already forgiven the offender each time you remember the debt and feel its catastrophic or collateral damage, soon, the memory of the debt will not produce the same feelings and anxieties as it did before. It will lose its power. This is the reason healing is often viewed as a process.

What Does Healing Look Like?

How can you be sure that you are healing? Healing and change can be measured from both a negative and positive perspective. Look back at your behavior before the journey. Another person can help mark your progress.

Consider your reactions in terms of frequency, duration, and intensity. You might remember that your inappropriate reactions were frequent. Perhaps the impact of a situation lasted for hours, days, months, or even years. The intensity of the event could have been a ten-plus on a scale of ten.

Now, what about the new you? Is the frequency of the negative reactions less frequent? Are your positive reactions more prevalent? The longer duration of the negative reactions might be replaced with abbreviated appropriate responses. You might also sense that the intensity of the situation has become considerably well below ten.

Healing brings more frequent positive responses over a period of time. The previous negative intensity might be replaced with the positive response of God's love. Measuring frequency, duration, and intensity, helps and you recognize healing and growth and encourages you to begin to live the resurrection life.

A Time for Reflection

1. What is the payment that satisfies all sin debt?

2. How is it possible to forgive someone who is not sorry?

3. What action are you called to take in the journey of forgiveness?

4. What needs to happen when you remember the hurt?

5. Explain why forgiveness can be considered both a one-time transaction and a process.

6. Define primary damage and collateral damage.

LIVING A RESURRECTION LIFE

The steps of resurrection in the journey of forgiveness are exciting. To get to this point, there might have been more than you imagined. The emotions felt overwhelming and debilitating. Yet, during the toughest of times, many discover a sense of hopefulness and strength. The resurrection life becomes more of a way of life than the simple practical steps of a process. Resurrection life is the wonderful new life you experience when you are free from the bondage of the offenses of others against you.

What If You Don't Feel Better?

Maybe you tried all the steps and still do not feel any better. Possibly, you feel worse. It takes time for healing and the fruit of righteousness to appear. Be patient and faithful.

Let us take a moment to discuss the most critical and active ingredient in the journey: Jesus. This is a spiritual journey. It might be hard to distinguish between trying to forgive in a human sense and a spiritual journey. Cooperation with God is vital on the journey. It is possible to cooperate with God when you have a trusting relationship with Him. This relationship has been made possible because of Jesus's death. If you crave healing, He is your Great Physician.[72] If you desire comfort, He is your Comforter.[73] If you seek advice, He is your Counselor.[74] If you seek to live in a state of wonder and awe, free from worry and anxiety, He is Wonderful; He is your Prince of Peace.

The painful tragedy of another's sin against you has brought you to earnestly desire certain things in your soul. You have fallen short and hurt the heart of your Holy God.[75] You too have missed the mark. You are called by God to seek forgiveness from Him and place your faith in what the Messiah has done to forgive all sin. Consider if you have ever trusted in what Jesus has done. The One who offended no one chose to die for all those who do offend. Have you acknowledged your sin and the price that was paid for it? If you have never come to the cross of forgiveness, you can pray in sincerity now, "Oh, Heavenly Father, I now recognize my need of forgiveness and ask Jesus to be my Savior. I pray in the name of Jesus; the name which causes you to hear my prayer. Amen."

Your Resurrection Life

This relationship with God provides the opportunity for a new life. The new life you found in Christ has been described as the incredible joy of your salvation,[76] and it is your sanctification. With growth and learning, understanding will increase. Sanctification is the work of God that provides the ability and power to live your Christian life. Sanctification is a moment-by-moment choice that requires you to believe what God has said. Therefore, though you choose the joy of extending forgiveness, it does not mean the next time will be "no problem." Each time, each choice, you must look to Jesus to receive from Him the faith and grace to give forgiveness that frees you from the inside out.[77] This moment-by-moment and circumstance-by-circumstance power enables you to realize it is never you. It is always God who is the author of love, goodness, and forgiveness. Your forgiveness of another human being is living, freeing, and joyful power. It is super-excellent joy. It is peace, the peace which passes all understanding.[78] It is grace, the grace which is all-sufficient.[79] It is a personal gift from God to you, the gift of genuine serenity. Joy will be restored.[80] It is the reality of intimacy with God and others. It is the ability to express your love to God and others as never before without the thought of reward. It is to receive and give unconditional love, accept from God, and give to others. It is His agape love. This supernatural celebration is experienced both in heaven and on earth.

Your resurrection life, which is the life of Christ living in you through the Holy Spirit, brings new awareness, insight, discernment, and balance. It cannot help but be so. It is no longer you but He who lives in you. You might suddenly become aware that in the same situation that previously caused you to overreact, you respond in an appropriate and kind manner. The intense struggles you dealt with in relationships subside. You have a sense of courage and boldness you never knew before. You possess a new way to relate to others. And you love it. You are experiencing characteristics of the resurrection life.

Five Characteristics of the Resurrected Life

(From Appendix D)

1. You enjoy being soft and tender toward yourself and others.

2. You sense a deepened compassion to respond to others from your soul.

---

3. You are free to make difficult and unpopular decisions that, in the past, would have been avoided.

4. You live life to its fullest through the power of the Holy Spirit.

5. You have victory over the inappropriate reactions of your past.

The Christian life will become an adventure for you. The Holy Spirit leads, and you follow. He lives in you, and He walks with you. You allow His words, actions, and response to fill your heart and soul and mind. Now you desire His ways more than you want your own way. You are living the truth of the following verse. "I am crucified with Christ: nevertheless I live; yet not I, but Christ lives in me: and the life which I now live in the flesh I live by the faith of the Son of God, who loved me, and gave himself for me" (Galatians 2:20).

As you begin to build a wonderful, intimate relationship with Christ, He enables you to do the same with others. Spiritual healing enables you to experience and express God's love in a way you could never comprehend before.

In this modern world, true love is often misunderstood. Many people expect that true love will leave them with a fulfilling sense of self-gratification. Although often accompanied by gratifying feelings, this is not the highest form of love. Godly love was demonstrated by the obedience of Jesus Christ to give His life so that you could know the love of His Father, your Father. In the same way as you give away your life, you will find it in Christ.

Obedient, giving love is defined as self-sacrifice for the undeserving that opens the door to restoration with the Father, with others, and with self. This love is described in

1 Corinthians 13, the universally recognized love chapter of the Bible. Again, you cannot manufacture this love. It can only be accomplished when you personally believe that God is in you and can perform His love through you. Only as you see yourself to be dead and Christ to be alive will He have full reign so that you can experience spiritual and emotional growth and maturity.

You are completely dependent upon Christ. To acknowledge this fact releases His power onto your life. To resist keeps you in the pattern of a defeated lifestyle. This love is alive in you and makes itself evident because it is Christ's love. He is living in you through the Holy Spirit.

The parable of the Good Samaritan[81] graphically illustrates the love that God desires for you to have for those around you. God has commanded you live out this form of love in practical ways toward the lovable daily; the unlovable; and yes, even toward your enemies.[82] This might seem unreasonable unless you have first experienced God's love through salvation and growth. To receive the forgiveness is the first requirement in learning to love others as God has loved you.

If you do not express Christlike love toward others, perhaps it is an indication that you need growth on the journey toward forgiveness. Please allow uncomfortable feelings to be indicators of the need to pursue a deeper relationship with Jesus Christ. Do not ridicule or condemn yourself, and do not listen to the judgments of others. Emotional energy is precious and needs to be directed toward progress in your spiritual pilgrimage. Consider ugly and uncomfortable feelings God's counsel and gift. They warn you of danger and help you recognize your need for further help and counsel. Be willing to seek out and accept such help from Him and others. The sincere prayer of a child of God is very productive.[83] There is safety in the multitude of counselors.[84] In contrast, if you suppress your feelings, you will not prosper.[85] If you lack the courage or ability to travel this journey, pray for the grace you need. God hears your prayers and promises to answer.

Five Internal Evidences of Healing (From Appendix E)

1. The intense emotional distress you once felt is now lessened.

2. The thought of the offender doesn't provoke anxiety or panic.

3. Being in the offender's presence doesn't rattle you.

4. You feel love toward the offender, not anger.

5. You are genuinely concerned for the offender's well-being.

Evidence of Growth

As you travel the path of forgiveness, there are specific internal evidences of growth. The relief from emotional distress is a welcomed gift. Your automatic responses no longer include the overreactions of rage, anxiety, and panic. Thoughts of the offender or the anticipation of being in his presence do not create the great tension of stress you were familiar with for so long. You begin to feel a genuine love for the offender and a heartfelt concern for his well-being.

The freedom and celebration that come when you experience the resurrection life will make it all worthwhile. The abundant life Christ died to provide for you will be God's gift to you as His dear and treasured child.

You might find yourself with a tremendous sense of gratitude and appreciation. Relish the moment. Praise God from whom all blessings flow. It has been a long journey with much more ahead. By this point, you want to share experience and joy. Please do, but do it thoughtfully. Remember how difficult it was at the beginning for you. To share your experience keeps it alive, fresh, and growing. Do not be forceful, but always be ready to give.

Ready to Give

Be ready to give love.

Be ready to give acceptance.

Be ready to give comfort.

Be ready to give support.

Be ready to give understanding.

Be ready to give forgiveness.

Be ready to give encouragement.

Be ready to give hope.

Be ready to give validation.

But be ready, because once you start giving, you will continue to receive back. Do not allow yourself to be drained, but give with a full heart. You will find it is more blessed to give than receive.[86] Wow! What a resurrection life!

A Time for Reflection

1. Have you prayed to ask Jesus to be your personal Savior?

2. Make a list of the old out-of-control reactions you experienced before the healing journey began and that you now want to eliminate from your life.

3. Describe the godly responses that you desire to replace old reactions.

4. Ask God to reveal His desires for you regarding questions two and three above.

5. List new patterns of behavior (a transformed life), and share how you reacted different before and after your journey of forgiveness. Celebrate!

What About Restitution?

An offense creates a debt. Restitution is payment for the damage caused by the offense. When forgiveness is granted, you recognize the full scope of the damage and declare the debt no longer exists. You consider it paid in full, erased, eradicated, no longer owed. Forgiveness does not mean there was no debt or that the debt has no value. In fact, in order to erase the debt, value needs to be established in the first place.

For example, if you purchased $1,000 of furniture by credit card, the debt would be placed on your account. You now owe $1,000. It is your debt. Suppose the credit card company informed you that you won a contest and no longer owed the $1,000. Your obligation has been paid in full. The credit card company would actually cancel a debt you rightfully owed. Your creditor cannot cancel the $1,000 debt unless he recognizes and declares the value of the credit card debt to be $1,000.

The Forgiver

When a person chooses to extend forgiveness, he releases the obligation from the offense and does not demand or expect any payment for the debt. Forgiveness declares that the debt no longer exists; it has been canceled, erased. The forgiver also commits himself not to hold resentments, shame, or guilt the offender. There are times, however, when another authority might step in and impose consequences, demand punishment, or require restitution. The legal system holds the offender responsible for his actions in the event of a criminal offense even when the violated individual forgives the offender.

Restitution cannot be made for many offenses. Emotional wounds and sexual violations are such an example. Preventing further injury is always a major concern. Whether or not restitution can be made is not the primary issue. Either way, the debt is canceled. Forgiveness is granted. Forgiveness is not forgiveness if it is determined by restitution. The injured party offers forgiveness whereas the offender offers restitution.

The Offender

Unfortunately, there are many occasions when the offender has no interest in offering restitution. On the other hand, there are occasions when an offender does desire and offer restitution for his offenses. Sometimes guilt encourages a repentant heart. At other times, an offender responds with a heart attitude of appreciation because of the mercy and grace of the forgiver. The desire to make restitution might be clear evidence of genuine sorrow and true repentance.[87]

There are many kinds of debts where a form of restitution might be possible, at least to some degree. Restitution shows the offender's genuine sincerity and interest in repairing the relationship. The forgiver should not determine it because the debt has been canceled. Restitution is the choice and determination of the offender. This is not to suggest that the offender would not consider the concerns of the forgiver. The benefit of restitution is that it becomes part of the offender's repentance and growth in responsibility. Fulfilling the obligation caused by the offense can work powerfully in the life of the offender.

When Restitution Becomes Grace

When restitution is offered, the forgiver might accept it if he chooses. Actually, because the debt has already been canceled, it becomes a gift from the repentant offender. There is no obligation for the injured to accept restitution. It might be appropriate to graciously decline restitution when the injured person needs time and separation to recover from the offense.

Offering restitution might help the offender in his effort to change. Tremendous transformation takes place when the violator becomes a generous and gracious protector and begins to learn and pass on grace appropriately.

Restitution also adds to the healing and growth of the injured person. Restitution acts as a public testimony of God's work in his life, which brings glory to God. Further, it can be a witness and encouragement to others who have been abused. It demonstrates change in the lives of both the offender and the offended. This offers hope to those who think that nothing will ever change. It might also act as a deterrent to those who are currently abusive. It reminds them that there is a just God.

Be careful not to anticipate restitution as a motive for forgiveness. Restitution is not required to forgive. It rarely repairs an offense. It is only a genuine peace offering in an attempt to repay and fulfill the obligation of the one seeking resolution and reconciliation.

Questions Regarding Restitution

How should I respond if I think the restitution is a payoff? Should I evaluate the motives of the one making restitution? Be aware of what you see in others, especially those who hurt you. Only God can truly judge their motives. You are not responsible for the motives of other people. Be careful not to allow yourself to become vulnerable because the offender desires to make restitution. If it is not accompanied by a change in attitudes and actions, the relationship might not be safe for you. You can choose to accept restitution or to redirect it to another beneficiary. When you forgive the offender and he indicates no change in heart, he misses the benefit from the grace and mercy granted to him.

What different forms does restitution take? If there is property damage or financial loss, restitution is more obvious. Restitution for spiritual damage, emotional wounds, or physical injury is not possible. If acts of kindness are now given, it does not restore that which was damaged or taken from you. Only God binds up the brokenhearted. Nurturing acts of kindness are in order simply because this is God's natural standard for relationships.

What if I feel uncomfortable accepting the restitution? How do I understand my feelings and evaluate the situation? It is common to feel uncomfortable when you accept restitution. It has not been normal for the offender to behave toward you in this way before now. Change does not feel comfortable at first. In time, genuine acts of love and kindness become a new way of life for you and the offender. Be patient with yourself and with the truly repentant offender.

A Time for Reflection

1. Name some reasonable payments you feel are appropriate from your debtors. These might be verbal, behavioral, or financial.

2. Discuss these payments with your support person.

3. Are you willing to release your debtor from his debt?

4. Write down what you might say to release your debtor from his debt.

5. If the debtor chooses, allow him to make restitution of his own free will. However, do not pressure or manipulate him in any way to gain restitution. You have forgiven the debt.

_____

_____

_____

_____

_____

_____

_____

_____

_____

_____

_____

_____

_____

Reconciliation and Restoration

The ultimate goal and evidence of complete forgiveness is reconciliation and restoration of the relationship. A more excellent way emerges as a loving lifestyle. What might have been considered an impossible ideal gradually becomes more natural.

Reconciliation means to resume a safe and godly manner of relating. Restoration occurs when two people enter back into the relationship as it was before the offense. A mutual relationship can be established after the offense is forgiven. Appropriate and meaningful interactions are experienced when forgiveness is complete. There are some reconciled relationships that are not appropriate to restore. For example, when a couple divorces and both parties remarry. It would honor God for them to reconcile with each other. This also would help the children involved. But because each spouse has remarried, the marriage relationship itself cannot be restored.

There are circumstances that might not allow for restoration to ever take place. If your journey of forgiveness led you to forgive someone who died, you cannot restore that relationship. However, it is possible to relate to that person in the way you talk about him or her. You can reconcile by speaking about him in an appropriate manner with others who knew him. Perhaps reconciliation is evident in the way you respond to others that remind you of this person or situations of the past. God fully understands reconciliation and restoration. He knows what is and is not possible.

There are times when it is unwise to restore. If the relationship was abusive and the abuser has not changed, it is unsafe to attempt to restore it. You can reconcile by establishing the relationship with distance and safe boundaries to protect you from further harm. This also allows less access for the opportunity for the offender to continue his sin toward you. As appropriate behavior is demonstrated, you may take some calculated small risks in order to determine if a closer relationship might be safe. You are to be willing, available, and open to restoration if and when the perpetrator cooperates. You are not obligated to jeopardize your safety at the mercy of an inappropriate abuser. There are also situations in which the other person was not abusive but involved in actions that were and are detrimental to your spiritual maturity or your emotional well-being. To restore relationships of this kind is not always a wise choice.

When people are malicious and do not behave appropriately, you do not have to put yourself in a situation that guarantees more injury. This does not imply that forgiveness has not been granted. It only means that restoration is not possible at this time. The offender needs to come to true repentance before the reconciled relationship can be restored. You are not responsible for the offender's responses at any point in your journey toward forgiveness. You are only called to forgive and love him regardless of his choices.

It has been said that forgiveness and love are opposite sides of the same coin. To love is to forgive; to forgive is to love. Even if a reconciled relationship cannot be restored, you can rejoice in your emotional healing and spiritual growth. You are free to enjoy the fruits of forgiveness. May you do so on a daily basis.

Chapter Fifteen

A Time for Reflection

1. Identify any relationships of the past or present that are not safe to reconcile.

2. Identify any relationships from the past or present that are not possible to restore.

3. Grant genuine forgiveness to those who have offended you. Describe the appropriate boundaries are necessary to protect yourself from further injury.

APPENDICES

A. Forms of Abuse

"Get rid of all bitterness, rage and anger, brawling and slander, along with every form of malice. Nor should there be obscenity, foolish talk or coarse joking, which are out of place, but rather thanksgiving" (Ephesians 4:31, 5:4).

Abuse comes in many forms:

> **Physical Abuse:** all displays of violence or threatening behavior.

> **Verbal Abuse:** any communication that interrupts, name-calls, insults, criticizes, condemns, degrades, ridicules, uses a harsh or sarcastic tone, or superlatives (uses such expressions such as "You always," "You never," "Every time").

> **Emotional Abuse:** behavior that controls, manipulates, ignores, minimizes or maximizes, threatens, dismisses, abandons, overwhelms, is rude, or teases. (Because fun is only fun when it is fun for everyone. If it's not fun for everyone, it's abuse.)

> **Sexual Abuse:** "any activity, verbal, visual, or physical, engaged in, without consent, which may be emotionally or physically harmful and which exploits one person in order to meet another person's sexual or emotional needs. The person does not consent if he or she cannot reasonably choose or consent or refuse because of age, circumstances, level of understanding, and dependency or relationship to the offender."[88]

B. Questions for the Healing Journey

These questions may be used over and over again for each incident and for each person involved in an offense.

"He who conceals his sins does not prosper, but whoever confesses and renounces them finds mercy" (Proverbs 28:13).

Q1: What was the incident? (A topic sentence.)

Q2: What do I remember about the incident? (Tell the full story.)

Q3: Who hurt me?

Q4: How was I hurt?

Q5: How did this hurt impact my life then?

Q6: How does this hurt impact my life now?

Q7: How might this hurt impact my life in the future?

C. THE FIVE COMMITMENTS OF FORGIVENESS

Modified from: The Peacemaker, Responding to Conflict Biblically, Institute for Christian Conciliation, Billings, Montana, 1996

Matthew 6:12; 1 Corinthians 13:5; Ephesians 4:32

1. I will not think about this incident *without also remembering the grace and forgiveness I extended to the offender.* (Italicized clarification by Steven R. Silverstein.)

2. I will not bring this incident up and use it against the offender.

3. I will not talk to others about this incident *unless talking about it will be an opportunity to glorify God for His healing work in my life or the life of others.* (Italicized clarification by Steven R. Silverstein.)

4. I will not allow this incident to stand between us or hinder our personal relationship. *In fact, I will seek to use the grace present as a catalyst for a more godly relationship.* (Italicized clarification by Steven R. Silverstein.)

5. *I will seek to understand the offender and show compassion.* (Added by Steven R. Silverstein.)

D. Five Characteristics of the Resurrection Life

1 Corinthians 13:4-8; Galatians 5:22-23

1. You enjoy being soft and tender toward yourself and others.

2. You sense a deepened compassion to respond to others from your soul.

3. You are free to make difficult and unpopular decisions that you would have avoided in the past.

4. You live life to the fullest.

5. You have victory over your inappropriate reactions of the past.

E. Five Internal Evidences of Healing

Rejoice in the Lord always. I will say it again: Rejoice! Let your gentleness be evident to all. The Lord is near. Do not be anxious about anything, but in everything, by prayer and petition, with thanksgiving, present your requests to God. And the peace of God, which transcends all understanding, will guard your hearts and your minds in Christ Jesus. (Philippians 4:4-7)

1. The intense emotional stress begins to ease.

2. The thought of the offender doesn't provoke anxiety or pain.

3. The presence of the offender doesn't rattle you.

4. You experience feelings of compassion toward the offender, not anger.

5. You are genuinely concerned for the offender's well-being.

F. THE HEALING JOURNEY OF FORGIVENESS

1. **Confess the Damage:** Acknowledge that offenses occurred in your life. (Appendix A.) (Matthew 18:7; Proverbs 28:13; 1 John 1:7-9.)

2. **Calculate the Destruction:** Recognize these offenses created a spiritual debt. (Appendix B.) (Matthew 18:23, 24, and 26-28.)

3. **Cancel the Debt:** Forgiveness means to erase the spiritual indebtedness. (Appendix C.) (Matthew 6:12; Matthew 18:21-35.)

4. **Confront the Debtor:** Spiritual wellness is connected to our obedience to Scripture and is in direct proportion to the degree of confrontation. (Matthew 5:24, 18:15.)

5. **Construct the Deflector:** A safe environment must be established to protect from future offenses. (1 Corinthians 3:16, 17; 1 Corinthians 6:20.)

6. **Consecrate the Diamond:** Experience the sanctifying work of God. (Appendix D and E.) (Leviticus 11:44; 1 Peter 1:16.)

7. **Clearing My Own Indebtedness.** (Appendix H.)

G. Help for the Hurting Heart

A guide to help you when you come alongside hurting people.

"The Spirit of the Lord GOD is upon me; because the Lord hath anointed me to preach good tidings unto the meek; he hath sent me to *bind up the brokenhearted*, to proclaim liberty to the captives, and the opening of the prison to them that are bound," (Isaiah 61:1).

1. **Compassion:** Be kind, gentle, tenderhearted, and sincere. (Ephesians 4:32; 1 Corinthians 13:4-8; Galatians 5:22, 23.)

2. **Consideration:** Consider the experience of the other person. Encourage him to share his concerns, thoughts, and feelings. Listen carefully without judgment, hear, and understand the person and the problem that is causing his/her heart to hurt. (2 Corinthians 1:2-4; Romans 12:15.)

3. **Consolation:** Give validation and acknowledgement that the person has been hurt and is in pain. You may acknowledge that you are aware of your own pain. (Psalm 31:9-10; Romans 12:15.)

4. **Construction:** Offer support and nurture a godly relationship by meeting legitimate needs. Consider establishing boundaries that offer protection from further injury. (Galatians 6:1-2.)

H. HEALING FOR THE HURTING HEART

A guide to help you when you come to reconcile with a person you have hurt.

"Therefore, if you are offering your gift at the altar and there remember that your brother has something against you, leave your gift there in front of the altar. *First go and be reconciled* to your brother; then come and offer your gift" (Matthew 5:23-24).

1. **Compassion:** Be kind, gentle, tenderhearted, and sincere. (Ephesians 4:32; 1 Corinthians 13:4-8; Galatians 5:22-23.)

2. **Consideration:** Consider the experience of the other person. Listen carefully, hear and understand the person and the problem that has caused his/her pain. (2 Corinthians 1:2-4; Romans 12:15.)

3. **Confession:** Acknowledge the person's pain. Admit and accept responsibility for your offences without excuse or explanation. (1 John 1:9; Matthew 18:7, 15, 21, and 35.)

4. **Cultivation:** Pursue and nurture a godly relationship by meeting legitimate needs. (1 Corinthians 13:7-8; Galatians 6:1-2.)

5. **Cancellation:** Express genuine sorrow. Commit to learn and practice new behavior. Ask for forgiveness and seek a response. Accept a negative response. (2 Corinthians 7:10; Matthew 5:23-24.)

6. **Consolation:** Ask permission to express love and affection verbally and physically. (Ephesians 4:32.)

GLOSSARY OF FEELINGS

Angry	Offended	Capable	Perfectionist	Distracted	Uncomfortable
Abused	Opposed	Challenged	Permissive	Divided	Undecided
Aggravated	Outraged	Charming	Persistent	Doubtful	Uneasy
Agitated	Patronized	Clever	Positive	Dubious	Unpredictable
Anguished	Peeved	Competitive	Prim	Enchanted	Unsettled
Annoyed	Perturbed	Concentrating	Proper	Fascinated	Unsure
Argumentative	Provoked	Convincing	Proud	Flustered	Vulnerable
Betrayed	Quarrelsome	Cooperative	Ready	Foggy	Worried
Bitter	Rage	Courageous	Resourceful	Foolish	
Cheated	Rebellious	Daring	Responsible	Frantic	**Happy**
Combative	Repulsed	Demanding	Reverent	Frustrated	Accepting
Condemned	Resentful	Demure	Right	Gullible	Acknowledged
Controlled	Resentment	Detailed	Serious	Hesitant	Adaptable
Coerced	Revengeful	Determined	Settled	Hysterical	Adequate
Cruel	Ridiculed	Eager	Sexy	Immobilized	Admired
Deceived	Sabotaged	Energetic	Show-off	Inconsistent	Adventurous
Destructive	Seething	Expert	Smart	Indecisive	Alive
Disagreeable	Short-tempered	Fighter	Solemn	Infatuated	Animated
Disgusted	Smothered	Forceful	Solid	Misunderstood	Appreciated
Displeased	Spiteful	Free	Strong-willed	Mystical	Assured
Disturbed	Stifled	Full	Studious	Naïve	Blissful
Dominated	Strangled	Good	Successful	Numb	Captivated
Enraged	Stubborn	Hard-working	Sure	Nutty	Cheerful
Envious	Surly	Helpful	Sympathetic	Obsessed	Compassionate
Evil	Throttled	Honored	Tenacious	Paranoid	Confident
Exasperated	Ticked Off	Idealistic	Thoughtful	Perplexed	Considerate
Exploited	Unaffectionate	Independent	Tireless	Puzzled	Content

Flustered	Unfair	Innocent	Tolerant	Queer	Creative
Frustrated	Unsympathetic	Inspired	Wild	Reluctant	Delighted
Fuming	Used	Intelligent		Restless	Determined
Furious	Vehement	Inventive	**Confused**	Scatter-brained	Ecstatic
Harassed	Vengeful	Keen	Agony	Screwed-up	Elated
Hateful	Vindictive	Kind	Ambivalent	Sheepish	Electrified
Hostile	Wicked	Leader	Astounded	Shocked	Encouraged
Humiliated		Loving	Awkward	Slow	Energized
Incensed	**Confident**	Meditative	Baffled	Stagnant	Enjoy
Infuriated	Able	Mediator	Bewildered	Stunned	Enthusiastic
Insulted	Adamant	Messy	Bothered	Stupefied	Excited
Intolerant	Ambitious	Neat	Childish	Surprised	Exuberant
Irritated	Assertive	Nice	Constricted	Suspicious	Fancy
Jealous	Beautiful	Nonchalant	Curious	Tentative	Flattered
Mad	Bold	Orderly	Deep	Torn	Fortunate
Manipulated	Brave	Outspoken	Directionless	Trapped	Friendly
Manipulative	Busy	Patient	Disbelieving	Troubled	Fulfilled
Mean	Calm	Peaceful	Disorganized	Uncertain	Fun-loving
Happy (cont'd.)	Silly	Obstinate	Horrible	**Scared**	Threatened
Funny	Sociable	Prissy	Humbled	Afraid	Timid
Gay	Spontaneous	Selfish	Hurt	Alarmed	Tormented
Gentle	Spirited	Skeptical	Idiotic	Anxious	Uneasy
Glad	Talkative	Sly	Ignored	Appalled	Unsure
Good	Tender	Smug	Inadequate	Apprehensive	Vulnerable
Grateful	Terrific	Sneaky	Isolated	Awed	Worried
Gratified	Thoughtful	Spiteful	Left out	Bashful	
Groovy	Thrilled	Stingy	Loner	Cautious	**Wonder**
Happy	Tranquil	Stubborn	Lonely	Concerned	Admiration
Heavenly	Understood	Vengeful	Low	Constricted	Amazed
High	Validated		Melancholy	Defensive	Astonish
Hopeful	Valued	**Sad**	Miserable	Desperate	Attentive
Humble	Witty	Abandoned	Moody	Diffident	Awed
Humorous	Zany	Alienated	Mournful	Disabled	Curious

Appendix

Imaginative		Ashamed	Neglected	Doubtful	Desire
Inspiring	**Indifferent**	Bad	Odd	Dreadful	Dreamer
Joyful	Apathetic	Broken	Overlooked	Edgy	Marvel
Jubilant	Bored	Burdened	Pain	Fearful	Mysterious
Justified	Plain	Condemned	Pained	Frantic	Perplexed
Kicky		Contrite	Persecuted	Frightened	Sensational
Light-hearted	**Pride**	Crushed	Pessimistic	Guarded	Uncertain
Lively	Aggressive	Defeated	Pitiful	Guilty	Want
Lovable	Almighty	Dejected	Quiet	Helpless	
Loved	Arrogant	Demoralized	Regretful	Horrified	
Lovestruck	Better than	Depressed	Rejected	Impatient	
Loving	Bossy	Deserted	Remorse	Insecure	
Loyal	Cold	Despised	Reserved	Intimidated	
Marvelous	Comprising	Devastated	Sluggish	Jumpy	
Mischievous	Conceited	Diminished	Sorrowful	Nervous	
Naïve	Conspicuous	Disappointed	Sorry	Overwhelmed	
Optimistic	Critical	Discarded	Stupid	Panicky	
Patriotic	Culpable	Discouraged	Suffering	Perplexed	
Peaceful	Deceitful	Disgraced	Terrible	Petrified	
Playful	Demanding	Disheartened	Unappreciated	Reluctant	
Pleasant	Disagreeable	Disillusioned	Undisciplined	Shaken	
Pleased	Distasteful	Dismal	Uncared for	Shocked	
Popular	Eavesdropping	Distant	Unloved	Shy	
Pleasing	Fussy	Distraught	Unwanted		
Proud	Laconic	Distressed	Upset	Simple	
Refreshed	Lazy	Drained	Weepy	Skeptical	
Relaxed	Lecherous	Embarrassed	Withdrawn	Startled	
Relieved	Licentious	Empty	Worthless	Stunned	
Resolved	Loaded	Enervated	Wounded	Suspicious	
Respected	Lustful	Exhausted		Swamped	
Respectful	Maudlin	Grievous		Talkative	
Rewarded	Mischievous	Guilty		Tempted	
Satisfied	Naughty	Helpless		Tense	
Sensitive	Parsimonious	Hopeless		Terrified	

Endnotes

1 "But if anyone causes one of these little ones who believe in me to sin, it would be better for him to have a large millstone hung around his neck and to be drowned in the depths of the sea. "Woe to the world because of the things that cause people to sin! Such things must come, but woe to the man through whom they come!" (Matthew 18:6-7).

2 "What do you think? If a man owns a hundred sheep, and one of them wanders away, will he not leave the ninety-nine on the hills and go to look for the one that wandered off? And if he finds it, I tell you the truth, he is happier about that one sheep than about the ninety-nine that did not wander off. In the same way your Father in heaven is not willing that any of these little ones should be lost" (Matthew 18:12-14).

3 Matthew 18:21-35.

4 "If any of you lacks wisdom, he should ask God, who gives generously to all without finding fault, and it will be given to him. But when he asks, he must believe and not doubt, because he who doubts is like a wave of the sea, blown and tossed by the wind. That man should not think

he will receive anything from the Lord; he is a double-minded man, unstable in all he does" (James 1:5-8).

5 "Do not be anxious about anything, but in everything, by prayer and petition, with thanksgiving, present your requests to God. And the peace of God, which transcends all understanding, will guard your hearts and your minds in Christ Jesus" (Philippians 4:6-7).

6 "But now you must rid yourselves of all such things as these: anger, rage, malice, slander, and filthy language from your lips. Do not lie to each other, since you have taken off your old self with its practices and have put on the new self, which is being renewed in knowledge in the image of its Creator" (Colossians 3:8-10).

7 "Do not conform any longer to the pattern of this world, but be transformed by the renewing of your mind. Then you will be able to test and approve what God's will is his good, pleasing, and perfect will" (Romans 12:2).

8 Robert McGee, Search for Significance (Houston, Texas: Rapha Publishing, 1990).

9 "Forgive us our debts, as we also have forgiven our debtors" (Matthew 6:12).

10 "If I give all I possess to the poor and surrender my body to the flames, but have not love, I gain nothing" (1 Corinthians 13:3).

11 "And be not drunk with wine, wherein is excess; but be filled with the Spirit" (Ephesians 5:18).

12 "Because it is written, Be ye holy; for I am holy"(1 Peter 1:16).

13 "For we are his workmanship, created in Christ Jesus unto good works, which God hath before ordained that we should walk in them" (Ephesians 2:10).

14 "'For my thoughts are not your thoughts, neither are your ways my ways,' saith the Lord. 'For as the heavens are higher than the earth, so are my ways higher than you r ways, and my thoughts than your thoughts'" (Isaiah 55:8-9).

15 "And forgive us our debts, as we forgive our debtors" (Matthew 6:12).

16 "Behold, thou desirest truth in the inward parts: and in the hidden part thou shalt make me to know wisdom" (Psalm 51:6).

17 "'For I know the thoughts that I think toward you,' saith the LORD, 'thoughts of peace, and not of evil, to give you an expected end'" (Jeremiah 29:11).

18 "Henceforth there is laid up for me a crown of righteousness, which the Lord, the righteous judge, shall give me at that day: and not to me only, but unto all them also that love his appearing" (2 Timothy 4:8).

19 Dr. Dan B. Allender, Wounded Heart (Colorado Springs, CO: NAV Press, 1990).

20 These needs are met by parents who fulfill their responsibility to scriptural directives, such as bring your children up in the nurture and admonition of the Lord. See Ephesians 6:4.

21 Luke 15:11-32.

22 "Get rid of all bitterness, rage and anger, brawling and slander, along with every form of malice. Be kind and compassionate to one another, forgiving each other, just as in Christ God forgave you" (Ephesians 4:31-32).

23 "For he cares for you" (1 Peter 5:7b).

24 "The Spirit of the Lord GOD is upon me; because the LORD hath anointed me to preach good tidings unto the meek; he hath sent me to bind up the brokenhearted, to proclaim liberty to the captives, and the opening of the prison to them that are bound" (Isaiah 61:1).

25 "'For my thoughts are not your thoughts, neither are your ways my ways,' declares the LORD. 'As the heavens are higher than the earth, so are my ways higher than your ways and my thoughts than your thoughts.'" (Isaiah 55:8-9).

26 "There hath no temptation taken you but such as is common to man: but God is faithful, who will not suffer you to be tempted above that ye

are able; but will with the temptation also make a way to escape, that ye may be able to bear it" (1 Corinthians 10:13).

27 John Nieder and Thomas M. Thompson, Forgive and Love Again (Eugene, Oregon: Harvest House Publishers, 1991), pp. 109-115 paraphrased.

28 "He restores my soul" (Psalm 23:3a).

29 "Why do you look at the speck of sawdust in your brother's eye and pay no attention to the plank in your own eye? How can you say to your brother, 'Let me take the speck out of your eye,' when all the time there is a plank in your own eye? You hypocrite, first take the plank out of your own eye, and then you will see clearly to remove the speck from your brother's eye" (Matthew 7:3-5).

30 Luke 15:11-32.

31 "Be still, and know that I am God: I will be exalted among the heathen, I will be exalted in the earth" (Psalm 46:10).

32 "He restores my soul" (Psalm 23:3a).

33 "That he would grant you according to the riches of his glory, to be strengthened with might by his Spirit in the inner man" (Ephesians 3:14-19).

34 "He who conceals his sins does not prosper, but whoever confesses and renounces them finds mercy" (Proverbs 28:13).

35 "For lack of guidance a nation falls, but many advisers make victory sure" (Proverbs 11:14).

36 New Life Live (1-800-NEWLIFE), NANC (National Association of Neouthetic Counselors, 317-337-9100), and the AACC (American Association of Christian Counselors, 1-800-526-8673) are resources to find Christian counselors in your area. Don't assume that any counselor in the network will be the right one for you. Interview the person and try to be sure it is a good fit. If it does not feel right trust your instincts and try someone else.

37 "Heal me, O LORD, and I shall be healed" (Jeremiah 17:14a).

38 "For this reason, since the day we heard about you, we have not stopped praying for you and asking God to fill you with the knowledge of his will through all spiritual wisdom and understanding. And we pray this in order that you may live a life worthy of the Lord and may please him in every way: bearing fruit in every good work, growing in the knowledge of God, being strengthened with all power according to his glorious might so that you may have great endurance and patience, and joyfully" (Colossians 1:9-11).

39 "I love those who love me, and those who seek me find me" (Proverbs 8:17).

40 "Above all, love each other deeply, because love covers over a multitude of sins" (1 Peter 4:8).

41 "For we know him who said, 'It is mine to avenge; I will repay,' and again, 'The Lord will judge his people'" (Hebrews 10:30).

42 "If your brother sins against you, go and show him his fault, just between the two of you. If he listens to you, you have won your brother over" (Matthew 18:15).

43 "And Jesus answered him, 'The first of all the commandments is, Hear, O Israel; the Lord our God is one Lord: And thou shalt love the Lord thy God with all thy heart, and with all thy soul, and with all thy mind, and with all thy strength: this is the first commandment. And the second is like, namely this, Thou shalt love thy neighbor as thyself. There is none other commandment greater than these'" (Mark 12:29-31).

44 "But I say unto you, Love your enemies, bless them that curse you, do good to them that hate you, and pray for them which despitefully use you, and persecute you" (Matthew 5:44).

45 "And be not conformed to this world: but be ye transformed by the renewing of your mind, that ye may prove what is that good, and acceptable, and perfect, will of God" (Romans 12:2).

46 "I can do all things through Christ which strengthens me" (Philippians 4:13).

47 "Let us not become weary in doing good, for at the proper time we will reap a harvest if we do not give up" (Galatians 6:9).

48 "Above all else, guard your heart, for it is the wellspring of life" (Proverbs 4:23).

49 Henry Cloud and John Townsend, Boundaries (Grand Rapids: Zondervan, 1992). Check out their website: www.newlife.com.

50 Cynthia A. Kubetin and James Malloy, Beyond the Darkness, p. 3; quoted from *Hope for Victims of Sexual Abuse*, Robert McGee and Dr. Harry Schaumburg.

51 "Even if I caused you sorrow by my letter, I do not regret it. Though I did regret it— I see that my letter hurt you, but only for a little while— yet now I am happy, not because you were made sorry, but because your sorrow led you to repentance. For you became sorrowful as God intended and so were not harmed in any way by us. Godly sorrow brings repentance that leads to salvation and leaves no regret, but worldly sorrow brings death" (2 Corinthians 7:8-10).

52 (Modified from: The Peacemaker, Responding to Conflict Biblically, Institute for Christian Conciliation, Billings, Montana, 1996). The italicized is clarification by the author.

53 Ike Reighard, Pastor, NorthStar Church, Kennesaw, Georgia.

54 "The servant's master took pity on him, canceled the debt and let him go" (Matthew 18:27).

55 "Let us not become weary in doing good, for at the proper time we will reap a harvest if we do not give up" (Galatians 6:9).

56 "Heal me, O LORD, and I will be healed; save me and I will be saved, for you are the one I praise" (Jeremiah 17:14).

57 "If your brother sins against you, go and show him his fault, just between the two of you. If he listens to you, you have won your brother over" (Matthew 18:15).

58 "The words of a gossip are like choice morsels; they go down to a man's inmost parts" (Proverb 18:8).

59 "Instead, speaking the truth in love, we will in all things grow up into him who is the Head, that is, Christ" (Ephesians 4:15).

60 "In all my prayers for all of you, I always pray with joy" (Philippians 1:4).

61 "Those who oppose him he must gently instruct, in the hope that God will grant them repentance leading them to a knowledge of the truth" (2 Timothy 2:25).

62 "A gentle answer turns away wrath, but a harsh word stirs up anger" (Proverbs 15:1).

63 "Do not repay evil with evil or insult with insult, but with blessing, because to this you were called so that you may inherit a blessing" (1 Peter 3:9).

64 "Be strong and courageous. Do not be afraid or terrified because of them, for the LORD your God goes with you; he will never leave you nor forsake you" (Deuteronomy 31:6).

65 "If you love me, you will obey what I command" (John 14:15).

66 "Humble yourselves before the Lord, and he will lift you up" (James 4:10).

67 "And we know that all things work together for good to them that love God, to them who are the called according to his purpose" (Romans 8:28).

68 "So watch yourselves. If your brother sins, rebuke him, and if he repents, forgive him" (Luke 17:3).

69 "Give thanks in all circumstances, for this is God's will for you in Christ Jesus" (1 Thessalonians 5:18).

70 "As for zeal, persecuting the church; as for legalistic righteousness, faultless. But whatever was to my profit I now consider loss for the sake of Christ" (Philippians. 3:6-7).

71 "Therefore, the kingdom of heaven is like a king who wanted to settle accounts with his servants. As he began the settlement, a man who owed him ten thousand talents was brought to him" (Matthew 18:23-24).

72 "On hearing this, Jesus said, 'It is not the healthy who need a doctor, but the sick'" (Matthew 9:12).

73 "To the church of God in Corinth, to those sanctified in Christ Jesus and called to be holy, together with all those everywhere who call on the name of our Lord Jesus Christ—their Lord and ours: Grace and peace to you from God our Father and the Lord Jesus Christ. I always thank God for you because of his grace given you in Christ Jesus" (1 Corinthians 1:2-4).

74 "For to us a child is born, to us a son is given, and the government will be on his shoulders. And he will be called Wonderful Counselor, Mighty God, Everlasting Father, Prince of Peace" (Isaiah 9:6).

75 "For all have sinned and fall short of the glory of God" (Romans 3:23).

76 Psalm 51.

77 "Let us fix our eyes on Jesus, the author and perfecter of our faith, who for the joy set before him endured the cross, scorning its shame, and sat

down at the right hand of the throne of God"
(Hebrews 12:2).

78 "And the peace of God, which transcends all
understanding, will guard your hearts and your
minds in Christ Jesus" (Philippians 4:7).

79 "But he said to me, 'My grace is sufficient for
you, for my power is made perfect in weakness.'
Therefore I will boast all the more gladly about
my weaknesses, so that Christ's power may rest
on me" (2 Corinthians 12:9).

80 "For his anger lasts only a moment, but his favor
lasts a lifetime; weeping may remain for a night,
but rejoicing comes in the morning" (Psalm
30:5).

81 Luke 10:30-37.

82 Luke 6:27-36.

83 "For lack of guidance a nation falls, but many
advisers make victory sure" (Proverbs 11:14).

84 "Therefore confess your sins to each other and
pray for each other so that you may be healed.
The prayer of a righteous man is powerful and
effective" (James 5:16).

85 "He who conceals his sins does not prosper, but
whoever confesses and renounces them finds
mercy" (Proverbs 28:13).

86 "In everything I did, I showed you that by this kind of hard work we must help the weak, remembering the words the Lord Jesus himself said: 'It is more blessed to give than to receive'" (Acts 20:35).

87 "Yet now I am happy, not because you were made sorry, but because your sorrow led you to repentance. For you became sorrowful as God intended and so were not harmed in any way by us. Godly sorrow brings repentance that leads to salvation and leaves no regret, but worldly sorrow brings death" (2 Corinthians 7:9-10).

88 Cynthia A. Kubetin and James Malloy, Beyond the Darkness, p. 3; quoted from *Hope for Victims of Sexual Abuse*, Robert McGee and Dr. Harry Schaumburg.